PEN
AIR WARRIORS

Wing Commander Arijit Ghosh (retd), commissioned in December 1986 into the Administrative (Air Traffic Control) branch, served at numerous frontline Air Force bases in the north-east and along the western border, gaining first-hand experience of operations in these regions.

During his service career, he commanded four Indian Air Force units, including an Air Force Provost and Security Unit in the north-east at the height of insurgency, as well as an Airman Selection Centre.

He was the first officer to be posted in the Thar Desert to oversee the building of a new Air Force Base, 40 kms from the border.

Ghosh headed the prestigious Air Force Sports Control Board (equivalent to a State Sports Association) as secretary and worked internationally with elite-level athletes in different sports disciplines. He was part of the organizing committee for the Military World Games and the Commonwealth Games.

In addition, he headed Indian Armed Forces Sports contingents to World Military Championships overseas as chief of mission and served as the Asian representative on the Jury of Appeal at a world championship.

A former Ranji Trophy cricketer for the Services (left-handed opening batsman and wicketkeeper), Ghosh was the first IAF officer to become a Level B coach from the BCCI National Cricket Academy (NCA) and a BCCI match referee for domestic matches. He was one of a select few brothers worldwide who set an international record by scoring hundreds together in the same innings of a first-class match—a prestigious list that includes some of the most renowned siblings in international cricket.

A prolific writer, he has authored over a hundred articles for *Outlook*, covering topics ranging from international cricket to education, military history and personal memoirs.

Additionally, Ghosh is a corporate speaker and a guest lecturer on management for officers of PSUs like Coal India and the Mining, Geological and Metallurgical Institute of India (MGMI).

ADVANCE PRAISE FOR THE BOOK

'Deeply researched and narrated in simple language, these remarkable true stories fill a long-standing gap in Indian military aviation literature and satisfy the common man's curiosity about the Indian Air Force and leave him thirsting for more'—**Air Marshal Saju Balakrishnan, AVSM, VM, Commander-in-Chief, Andaman and Nicobar Command (CINCAN)**

'Wing Commander Arijit Ghosh has kept life simple as a worthy Air Force officer and an accomplished cricketer. As a veteran now, this simplicity in his writing makes him dear to the reader. Already a well-known sportswriter, Arijit has now taken on the much-needed work of reaching out to the next generation with a compilation of Air Warriors' stories, right from the "Birth of the Air Force" to the present day. A wonderful read!'—**Air Marshal Pramod V. Athawale, PVSM, AVSM, VSM, former Air Officer Commanding-in-Chief, HQ Maintenance Command, Indian Air Force**

'The USP of this book is the easy familiarity with which the author, who himself wore the Blue uniform for twenty-five years, talks about the protagonists and their incredible deeds. Some of them he had personally served with, and some were much respected seniors who welcomed him with the easy camaraderie that exists amongst all military personnel, comrades in arms, as they narrated their stories to him. Hard to put down!'—**Air Marshal R.C. Mahadik, AVSM, VSM, former Air Officer-in-Charge Administration, Indian Air Force**

'The common thread that runs through all the stories in this book is that it presents an intimate picture of different facets of the IAF and its people, in an engaging portrayal that catches and holds the reader's interest. The human-interest angle, often brought out through direct narratives recounted from the viewpoint of the actual protagonists, makes it a riveting read'—**Air Vice Marshal Prashant Karkare, VSM (retd), former Senior Officer-in-Charge Administration, HQ Western Air Command, Indian Air Force**

AIR WARRIORS

TRUE STORIES OF VALOUR AND COURAGE FROM THE INDIAN AIR FORCE

WING COMMANDER
ARIJIT GHOSH
RETD

PENGUIN
VEER

An imprint of Penguin Random House

PENGUIN VEER

Penguin Veer is an imprint of the Penguin Random House group of companies whose addresses can be found at global.penguinrandomhouse.com

Published by Penguin Random House India Pvt. Ltd
4th Floor, Capital Tower 1, MG Road,
Gurugram 122 002, Haryana, India

First published in Penguin Veer by Penguin Random House India 2024

Copyright © Arijit Ghosh 2024

All rights reserved

10 9 8 7 6 5 4 3 2 1

The views and opinions expressed in this book are the author's own and the facts are as reported by him which have been verified to the extent possible, and the publishers are not in any way liable for the same.

Please note that no part of this book may be used or reproduced in any manner for the purpose of training artificial intelligence technologies or systems.

ISBN 9780143465690

Typeset in Adobe Caslon Pro by Manipal Technologies Limited, Manipal
Printed at Thomson Press India Ltd, New Delhi

This book is sold subject to the condition that it shall not, by way of trade or otherwise, be lent, resold, hired out, or otherwise circulated without the publisher's prior consent in any form of binding or cover other than that in which it is published and without a similar condition including this condition being imposed on the subsequent purchaser.

www.penguin.co.in

Contents

Foreword   vii

Introduction   xi

1. Aces High—the Pioneers and the Birth of an Air Force (1917–1960)   1
2. The Bomber That Flew in from an Aircraft Graveyard (1948–1969)   21
3. The IAF in the 1962 War (1962)   44
4. Foes Turned Friends and the High-Flying Enemy (1965)   67
5. Hitting Sargodha and the Search for Flight Lieutenant Tapan Chaudhuri (1965)   85

6. Notes from the War Diary of a Fighter Controller (1971)   107

7. The Forming of the Thunderbolts (1981–1982)   125

8. The IAF in the Kargil Operations (1999)   148

9. Maldives Ahoy (2004)   164

10. Born and Raised in the IAF (1986–2010)   189

Epilogue   209

Acknowledgements   211

Foreword

'Few people realize that flying began in India as early as 1910, barely half a dozen years after the pioneering flights of Orville and Wilbur Wright at Kitty Hawk in the US. During World War I, several Indians joined the Royal Flying Corps and saw action on the Western Front.

Later, six young men, who made up the first batch of Indian flight cadets to be trained as pilots at RAF Cranwell, left for England in 1930, for a two-year flying training course. Another young Indian, 'Aspy' Engineer, followed them a few months later.

These men would script history and go on to build a brand new air force.

They were the pioneers who carved out a permanent niche for Indian pilots amongst the very best in the world. A place that the IAF continues to hold proudly, ninety-two years later, as the fourth largest air force of the world.'

Quoting these lines from the text seems to be the perfect way to begin this foreword to a book that traces the formation and proud history of the Indian Air Force, through true events from different periods in its glorious journey.

They talk intimately of men of great courage and grit, who endeavoured and succeeded against all odds, in building the mighty service that the IAF is today. Many of their names and incredible deeds are now forgotten, unknown to most of us, buried in the mists of time.

Set against the backdrop of life and day-to-day operations, these stories speak compellingly to readers in an easy, conversational manner and bring out the best of the Indian Air Force. Some of them have never been told before.

Technical terms and jargon have been kept to a minimum as the author, veteran Wing Commander Arijit Ghosh, who wore the blue uniform for twenty-five years, speaks with easy familiarity about life in the IAF, its aircraft and machines and the remarkable men behind them.

The free-flowing text brings old, long-forgotten incidents back to life, as he highlights the challenges, feelings and insights, and most of all, the understated courage of the men who actually lived those inspiring moments. This is a book about ordinary men who did extraordinary things.

They make us proud, even today, and that is why their stories need to be told, over and over again.

Happy reading!

Air Chief Marshal Arup Raha (R),
former chief of the Air Staff, IAF

Introduction

I was a cricketer who enjoyed writing. So when my playing days at Ranji Trophy and club-level ended, I naturally turned to writing about cricket. And that is how it remained for a while, as I enthusiastically churned out cricket articles for *Outlook* magazine.

Two things contributed in a big way to the writing of this book. One was my love and interest for flying, particularly the flying of the two World Wars. I grew up, like many other young boys of my generation, devouring the Biggles and Gimlet stories by Capt. W.E. Johns (not many would know of them now, I guess). And the illustrated War Picture Library books, depicting stories of World War II in pictures. To this day, they remain my 'comfort read' whenever I am able to lay my hands on one of these books, now becoming more and more difficult to find, as time goes by.

The second factor was that my dad was a great aficionado of Penguin Books, and we grew up in a house full of Penguin and Pelican Books dating right back to the World War II years, when compact 'Penguin Parade' and other compact pocketbooks were the rage. Probably because they could easily fit into the oversized pockets of World War II soldiers' uniforms, with the top flaps neatly buttoned down.

Those books would have offered a few rare moments of much-needed relaxation for weary soldiers unsure of whether they would witness the next sunrise.

Many of them were colour-coded—white with green borders for crime and detective, orange and white for general fiction, red and white for plays, dark blue and white for biographies, etc.

Dad had a handwritten letter from the founder and CEO of Pelican Books, Sir Allen Lane, which he treasured until the very end. In the letter, Sir Allen welcomed his interest in Penguin and described how he had started Penguin in 1935 in the crypt of Holy Trinity Church on Euston Road, London, using two empty tombs on which doors had been fitted.

From tiny acorns do mighty oaks grow, as the saying goes!

So when Penguin Veer offered me the chance to write a book of true stories from the Indian Air Force, thanks to an introduction from a young friend of mine, I jumped at the opportunity. Although, at that point, I did not really know what the book would be all about. The idea for it developed gradually as I talked to many friends from the Air Force, coursemates and seniors, including some whom I regarded as mentors, like Air Marshal P.V. Athawale. He was captaining the Air Force cricket team many moons ago when I was his vice-captain as a junior.

As the outlines of the stories developed in my mind, he introduced me to many people who had personally witnessed and participated in some of the events that I wanted to write about.

What followed were many long conversations, some with people well into their eighties, who were kind enough to give me their time and share their memories with me. Their ability to recall events long forgotten, in razor-sharp detail, amazed me.

Equally supportive were my family members—my wife Lipika and children Aniket and Nilanjana—who patiently allowed me the time to research and write and helped with editing whenever I asked.

And when it all seemed too overwhelming and I felt like I had bitten off more than I could chew, there were friends, some of whom I had known for fifty years, friends who had gone to kindergarten with me in a beautiful small town a lifetime ago, who pepped me up with the warmth of their support. Because of all these people, this book is a reality today, and I know I would never be able to thank them enough.

I am grateful also to the former Chief of Air Staff, Air Chief Marshal Arup Raha, who kindly consented to write the foreword to this book at short notice, and to the senior officers who said they had enjoyed the book and had nice things to say about it.

But most of all, to the protagonists of these true stories—who were the salt of the earth—it was a privilege to have worn the same uniform as them.

To each one of them, I raise a smart salute that my drill instructor at the Air Force Academy, Sergeant Andrews, would have been proud of, and wish them Blue Skies, Fair Winds and Happy Landings.

Jai Hind!

1

Aces High—the Pioneers and the Birth of an Air Force (1917–1960)

As he so often liked to do, nineteen-year-old Lieutenant Indra Lal Roy climbed into the wooden cockpit of his beloved square-nosed, single-seat SE 5a biplane (tail No. B180), and took off alone. It was early one July morning in 1918 with World War I still raging, as he flew over the battle-scarred trenches of France. The nose-mounted machine gun could fire through the propeller and there was a spare drum of ammunition mounted inside his cockpit. Soaring over the German-occupied French town of Carvin with the morning air smooth and still, this was his favourite time to fly. And hunt . . .

Fondly called 'Laddie' by his Squadron mates of 40 Squadron 'A' Flight, his boyish good looks belied his enviable reputation as an ace fighter pilot who had shot down ten enemy aircraft (two shared). Five of these were destroyed (one shared), and five 'down out of control' (one shared), in a little over 170 hours of flying time, in the space of just thirteen days.

Like many Air Aces of World War I, he loved to hunt alone, savouring the freedom of those solo forays in the war-torn skies over enemy lines that allowed for exceptional acts of individual bravery and courage. He trusted and leveraged to maximum effect his combat skills in dogfights with multiple German aircraft, including the mainstream Pfalz D.III and Fokker D.VII fighters that made up the backbone of their Air Force. Twice, he had shot down two enemy aircraft in a single combat sortie, and three on the same day once. As his score mounted and his reputation spread, he was feared and respected alike by his opponents.

This was his second tour of duty in France with the RFC, the Royal Flying Corps, that subsequently became the RAF, the Royal Air Force.

After his commissioning as a Second Lieutenant on 5 July 1917, he had been shot down and badly injured in December on his very first operational sortie with 56 Squadron, also equipped with SE 5a. So bad were his injuries that he had been given up for dead and put in a French mortuary, where he woke up subsequently and managed to get out by banging loudly on the door.

The terrified morgue staff called him the 'Boy from the Dead'.

He spent the next six months recuperating in a hospital during which time he made some beautiful sketches of military aircraft, some of which survive to this day, more than a 100 years later.

He returned to active duty in a ground job as an Equipment Officer. Lesser mortals would have been happy with that, but the fire of adventure and wartime fighter flying still burnt brightly in the nineteen-year-old, and he volunteered for, and soon cleared his medical exam for re-joining operational flying duties with in June 1918.

Laddie was soon back where he belonged, in the cockpit of his favourite S.E.5a fighter. And the rest, as they say, is history.

It seemed as if he were a man in a hurry to make up for lost time, as he shot down one enemy aircraft after other, starting with a Hannover C on 6 July. This was followed by three victories in the space of four hours on 8 July (two Hannover Cs and a Fokker D.VII); two on 13 July (a Hannover C and a Pfalz D.III); two on 15 July (two Fokker D.VIIs); and one on 18 July (a DFW C.V). His tenth and final victory came on 19 July when he shot down a Hannover C over Cagnicourt.

On 22 July 1918, a 106 years ago, Laddie Roy had taken off in search of his eleventh victim. Still little more than a young boy, one month shy of his twentieth birthday, he had been attending St Paul's school in Kensington, London, just a year ago. Now he was firmly established as one of the top allied air aces of the Great War, the War that was supposed to end all wars.

Everyone knows how hollow *that* claim turned out to be.

That fateful day, on 22 July 1918, as he patrolled the skies, alone in his S.E 5a fighter, high over enemy lines, did he at some point, have a premonition, a sense of foreboding like the Irish Airman in the famous W.B. Yeats war poem, and like him, feel, 'I know I shall meet my fate/ Somewhere among the clouds above /A lonely impulse of delight/ Drove to this tumult in the clouds', as he ran into a bunch of Fokker D VIIs of Jasta 29 (or 29 Fighter Squadron), of the Imperial German Air Service, as the Luftwaffe was called then.

Outnumbered and surrounded, he fought like a tiger using all the manoeuvring and dogfighting skills at his disposal, throwing loops and barrel rolls and Immelmann turns, as he sought to gain the upper hand in that raging, unequal dogfight. But the odds were just too great and there were just too many of them firing at him.

His aircraft went down in flames over the French town of Carvin, on the German side of the line. The crash killed him instantly, ending a short, but brilliantly luminous career as an ace fighter pilot on the Western Front, a month short of his twentieth birthday.

He had lasted a little over the expected average life span of fighter pilots on the Western Front, of about a month, shot down ten enemy aircraft and earned the respect of friend and foe alike, for his magnificent flying skills and courage.

Word spread quickly that a feared opponent and war hero was no more. The 'Tumult in the Clouds' driven by 'A lonely Impulse of Delight' had indeed come to an end.

The RAF honoured him with a DFC, the Distinguished Flying Cross (posthumous), the first Indian to be so honoured. He was buried at the Estevelles Communal Cemetery maintained by the Commonwealth War Graves Commission, where the headstone, interestingly, mentions his rank as a Flight Lieutenant (equivalent to a Captain in the army) of the RAF, instead of the Second Lieutenant's rank that he actually wore at the time . . .

The inscription simply reads, 'He died for the ideals he loved'.

The Indian Postal Department issued a commemorative postage stamp in his honour in 1998 to mark his 100th birth anniversary, and another one in 2018 to mark the 100th anniversary of his death. He remains the first, and till date, only Indian Air Ace, a title reserved for pilots who have shot down at least five enemy aircraft.

And in a later day salute to the young hero, it would be safe to say that Laddie's exploits inspired generations of Indian Air Force pilots over the years.

The Indian Air Force came into being in 1932 as the Royal Indian Air Force. In 1943, the first official Indian Air Force 'history' was brought out as a small thirty-page booklet called 'Ten Years Old' to mark the tenth anniversary of the raising of the IAF. This booklet was authored by Wing Commander W.W. Russell, a British officer who served with the IAF Volunteer Reserve and provides fascinating insights into the baby steps of the nascent Royal Indian Air Force (RIAF).

Few people realize that flying began in India as early as 1910, barely half a dozen years after the initial flights of Orville and Wilbur Wright at Kitty Hawk in the US. During World War I, several Indians joined the Royal Flying Corps (RFC) and saw action on the Western front. Lieutenant Indra Lal Roy was of course, the most celebrated and famous amongst them. Some of the other Indians who applied for a Commission in the RFC between November 1916 and April 1917, included Lieutenant Piroshaw Bomanjee Jeejeebhoy, Lieutenant Hardit Singh Malik who later became the Indian Ambassador to France, Lieutenant Shrikrishna Welinkar and Lieutenant Eroll Chunder Sen. Like Laddie Roy, twenty-three-year-old Lieutenant ShriKrishna Welinkar was shot down in aerial combat on 27 June 1918, less than a month before Roy's death, and was buried by the Germans in Belgium. Lieutenant Sen was luckier, he landed safely behind enemy lines after being shot down and was taken prisoner of war. He returned to India after the war.

These brave young men overcame prevalent western prejudices of the time that created many a hurdle for them before they actually took to the skies for the Royal Flying Corps and the RAF. They were the true pioneers of early Indian military aviation, even if they flew for a foreign flag.

They needed to first prove that they could fly as well as anyone else and were good leaders as well, before gaining grudging acceptance. And they will always have our highest admiration and regard for achieving that.

And like the BBC documentary on the young men who died in the Great War so poignantly says, 'They Shall Not Grow Old'.

For us.

Between 1914 and 1918, approximately 15 lakh Indians participated in World War I—by far the highest number of men from any of Britain's colonies or dominions at the time. Estimates put the number of Indians that died at around 70,000. How well these heroes acquitted themselves, in the face of mortal danger in a foreign land, in an alien environment! Their service is only now beginning to be acknowledged.

As the inscription on the wall of the Neuve-Chapelle Indian War Memorial in France says, 'Their name liveth for evermore' as it honours 4,742 Indian soldiers and labourers who died on the Western Front but have no known graves.

The Commonwealth War Graves Commission notes: 'over the course of the war, India sent over 1,40,000 men to the Western Front—90,000 serving in the infantry and cavalry and as many as 50,000 as non-combatant labourers. They hailed from the length and breadth of British India.'

They don't even talk about the RFC and the RAF because the numbers were too few. Yet, their contribution was no less significant.

At the inauguration of the Neuve-Chapelle Indian War Memorial after the War, the Commander-in-Chief of the Allied Forces in France, Marshal Ferdinand Foch, the French General who was one of the signatories to the armistice that ended the War in November 1918, said poignantly to a group of Indian servicemen who attended the ceremony, 'Return to your homes in the distant, sun-bathed East and proclaim how your countrymen drenched with their blood, the cold northern land of France and Flanders, how they delivered it by their ardent spirit from the firm grip of a determined enemy. Tell all India that we shall watch over their graves with the devotion due to all our Dead. We shall cherish above all the memory of their example. They showed us the way, they made the first steps towards the final victory.'

These men deserve our highest acclaim. Sadly, very few know of them today.

The glorious legacy of Laddie Roy passed on to his equally illustrious nephew, Subroto Mukerjee, who was amongst the first batch of six cadets to join the Royal Indian Air Force, twelve years after the Great War ended. They did their flying training at RAF Cranwell in the UK and Subroto subsequently rose to become the first Indian Chief of the Indian Air Force, as an Air Marshal. He won a DSO, the Distinguished Service Order (Military Wing), for distinguished service as a Flight and Squadron Commander in World War II, living up to his maternal uncle's glittering legacy in the Great War.

Another illustrious Royal Indian Air Force Pilot, Wing Commander K.K. 'Jumbo' Mazumdar, also from amongst the initial batches of Indian cadets who trained in the UK, went on to win a DFC and Bar (which means he was awarded the DFC twice). A very rare honour indeed, for his fearless and distinguished service in World War II.

He became the highest-ranking Indian Air Force officer of the time, when he attained the rank of Wing Commander during the Second World War, the first Indian to do so. In a unique honour, the magazine *Life* named him amongst the twelve greatest aviators of World War II.

This is the story of those magnificent men in their flying machines, who were instrumental in paving the way for the birth of the Indian Air Force, proving in no uncertain terms, the mettle of Indian pilots to the world. Today, in its ninety-second year of existence, as the fourth largest air force in the world, it is only right that we take a moment to look back at the early years of that glorious journey, especially at some of the icons who pioneered it and played pivotal roles in establishing a proud and illustrious legacy.

Without exception, they looked upon military flying as a passion and an adventure, and blazed a trail that generations would follow, breaking down barriers and prejudices, and establishing an air force that grew from strength to strength.

Coincidentally, all three came from the Indian city of Calcutta, now called, Kolkata. And tragically, all three died overseas, very young, the first one a month shy of his twentieth birthday when he was shot down in World War I. The second, in an accident at forty-nine years of age, while the third was just thirty-one when he crashed while performing aerobatics at an air show in Lahore.

The birth of a new enterprise is usually greeted with much scepticism and doubt, except amongst the few who can envision what others cannot. This was true of the formation of the IAF too. A few wise men of great foresight visualized what seemed a flight of fancy at the time, a mere fantasy to most. That of an air force of many squadrons, officered by Indians, maintained by Indians, earning the same respect that the Indian Army had earned from its brothers-in-arms.

It would have remained the stuff of dreams, but for the courage and enthusiasm of six young men, who made up the first batch of Indian Flight Cadets to be trained as pilots at RAF Cranwell.

H.C. Sirkar, Subroto Mukerjee, Bhupendra Singh, A.B. Awan, Amarjit Singh and Jagat Narain Tandon left for England in 1930 for a two-year flying training course at RAF Flying College, Cranwell. Another young Indian, 'Aspy' Engineer, followed them a few months later. These men would script history and go on to build a brand-new Air Force.

To quote from that first Indian air force 'history' of thirty pages mentioned above, 'these young Indians were not only starting a new life in a new country but were laying the foundations of a new Air Force: an Air Force which existed on paper alone at the time, and which many believed would never materialize into the complex organization of men, aeroplanes and equipment, which goes to make up a modern army of the air.'

At Cranwell, the six Indian Flight Cadets were amongst the pick of sportsmen and quickly made a name as they settled down and steadily gained acceptance and even admiration. H.C. Sirkar captained the hockey team which also had A.B. Awan, Amarjit Singh and Subroto Mukerjee in the side. Amarjit Singh captained the tennis team with two other Indians playing on it.

On the flying side, Aspy Engineer, who was to later become the second Indian Air Force Chief after the sudden and unfortunate demise of Air Marshal Subroto Mukerjee, was the only man with previous flying experience amongst the six. He had flown all the way from India to England and back, in a single-engine Tiger Moth. For this daring transcontinental flight, he had won the prestigious Aga Khan Prize. In those pioneering days of aviation, a cross-country flight of 5000 miles in a light, single-engine aircraft, which included a crossing of the Mediterranean, was a feat that not many would have dared to attempt.

At Cranwell they had their fair share of adventures and Aspy featured prominently in them, particularly when he had to bale out with his aircraft on fire, while practising aerobatics. He won the prestigious Grove Memorial Prize for the best all-round pilot of his term.

After the course, the Indian pilots trained at the Army Cooperation School at Wiltshire, and then served a short internship with a RAF squadron, before returning home to embark on their momentous journey of building an Indian Air Force.

All of them joined the newly formed No. 1 Squadron of the Royal Indian Air Force in April 1933.

Other flight cadets from India soon followed the first batch. Their names are now part of the legend and history of the Indian Air Force. They included K.K. Jumbo Majumdar, who commanded No. 1 Squadron in Burma where he won his first DFC, Henry Runganadhan, Prithipal Singh, Narendra, 'Bulbul' Khan, and Mehar Singh. And of course, there were Arjan Singh, the beloved 'Marshal of the Indian Air Force' of later years, Ravinder Singh and S.N. Goyal, all of whom passed through Cranwell and returning to India were posted to No. 1 Squadron.

On 1 April 1933, 'A' Flight, or the first flight of the No. 1 Squadron, Indian Air Force, was formed at Drigh Road, Karachi. Pilot Officer Subroto Mukerjee was among the five Indian pilots who made up the flight. It was commanded by Flight Lieutenant (later Air Vice Marshal) Cecil Bouchier DFC of the RAF and included a British Flying Officer and a number of British NCOs, since technical tradesmen who could work on the aircraft, were hard to find at the time.

The Westland Wapiti IIA or 'Wop', as it was popularly called, was the very first aircraft of the Royal Indian Air Force. Bought for a princely sum of ten pounds each, they were transferred from existing RAF Squadrons in India to the RIAF. The Wapiti was a two-seat, multi-role biplane with a top speed of 225 kilometres per hour and a flying range of 580 kilometres. It was used in a variety of roles by the RIAF, including escorting of convoys, anti-submarine patrols, air reconnaissance, strafing and bombing of ground targets.

An interesting feature of this aircraft was that the Observer/Gunner in the rear seat had to be chained to the floor of the aeroplane, since there was always a chance that he might fall out of the open cockpit during manoeuvres.

From those humble beginnings, the Indian Air Force, which started with six men and a single flight of four antiquated biplanes, is now in its 'nervous nineties', in its ninety-second year having grown to the hallowed status of the fourth largest air force in the world in the course of that journey. It has more than justified the vision and foresight of the men who sponsored its formation and the courage and enthusiasm of the young men who flew its first aeroplanes.

By the time World War II ended and India became independent, the IAF was well and truly established on the path of 'Touching the Sky with Glory' or 'Nabha Sparsham Diptam' as its motto proudly proclaims in Sanskrit.

Air Marshal Subroto Mukerjee is often called the 'Father and Architect of the Indian Air Force'. After the tragic loss of the Singh brothers (Amrajit Singh and Bhupinder Singh) in a Wapiti air crash at Quetta in 1933 and the departure of Flying Officer H.C. Sircar, who had to leave the service in 1935 as a result of a court martial for a horrific flying accident, Subroto Mukerjee, A.B. Awan (who later joined the Pakistan Air Force after World War II), and Aspy Engineer were the only Indian pilots left in the RIAF out of the original batch of Indian aviators. The government offered to absorb them in to the prestigious Indian Civil Service (ICS), provided they resigned from the RIAF. Subroto Mukerjee promptly rejected the offer knowing that its acceptance would mean the end of the young, fledgling Air Force.

And he was not about to let that happen. At any cost. Both he and his able second-in-command, Aspy Engineer, were men of great vision and foresight and together, they boldly decided in 1936, to introduce the revolutionary

Inter Community Messes in the Indian Air Force, where Hawai Sepoys, or personnel below officer rank, of all castes and creeds sat and dined together, something unheard of in those days.

And so, they demolished in one stroke, the seemingly insurmountable caste barrier and infused a spirit of integration and brotherhood amongst all ranks of the IAF. It was a daring experiment, one that could have led to the dismissal of these two young officers had it failed, in addition to other consequences, of which they had been warned by the RAF authorities.

Instead, the experiment proved to be a great success and the inter-community messes became living examples of the integration and brotherhood that has been the backbone of the IAF over the years.

By July 1938, No. 1 Squadron consisted of three flights and the Flight Commanders were Flying Officers Mukerjee, Engineer, and Majumdar. The outbreak of World War II saw the formation of the Coastal Defence Flights (CDFs) of the Indian Air Force Volunteer Reserve. In 1939, Subroto Mukerjee was promoted to Squadron Leader and in a very significant 'first', took over command of No. 1 Squadron, RIAF.

In the evolution of the IAF, Subroto was a man of innumerable firsts. He became the first Indian to command a flight, a squadron, a RAF Station (RAF Kohat in 1943), and finally the Indian Air Force, itself.

1 April 1954 was a red-letter day in the history of the Indian Air Force when Air Marshal Subroto Mukerjee

took over as the first Indian Chief of Air Staff of the IAF, marking a giant step forward for the new nation and its fledgling air force. Till then the IAF had been led successively by three British Chiefs.

Over the next six years Mukerjee oversaw many new ventures and advancements, as the service grew spectacularly under his leadership. The IAF became the first air force in Asia to acquire jet aircraft when Vampires were inducted into service, followed soon after by the Toofanis. These were followed by other state-of-the-art aircraft of the time, such as the Dassault Mystere IVAs, Hawker Hunters, English Electric Canberras, and Folland Gnats, laying the foundation of a modern air force.

The IAF looked forward to many more years of growth under his dynamic, yet empathetic leadership. However, it was not to be . . .

On an official trip to Japan, tragedy struck at a restaurant in Tokyo when he was having a meal with a friend from the Indian Navy.

The man who had survived a World War as a fighter pilot, choked on his food and before a doctor could be summoned, it was all over. With his shocking and untimely demise, the Indian Air Force had lost one of its founders and most illustrious officers.

A grateful service paid tribute in an impressive fly-past of forty-nine aircraft, one for each of his forty-nine years. It was one of the largest flypasts ever flown by the IAF, bettered only in 2022, by a seventy-five-aircraft display. As each aircraft dipped its wings in a poignant final salute to the 'father figure' of the air force, there were many moist eyes amongst the audience. Mukerjee's multi-faceted and dynamic, yet warm and caring personality had endeared him to everyone who knew him.

An example of that dynamism was his interest in sports. He envisioned a football tournament for school boys conducted by the IAF that he personally obtained permission for from then prime minister, Pandit Jawaharlal Nehru. Sadly, by the time the first edition of this tournament commenced in December 1960, he was no more, and the tournament was named the 'Subroto Cup' at Pandit Nehru's insistence.

Over the next sixty-three years, the Subroto Cup would assume iconic status as it grew from strength to strength and provided a wonderful platform and launching pad for many a young footballer who went on to play for the country with distinction. This was a perfect illustration of his perspective, foresight, and empathy for all.

Half a century later, as the Secretary of the Air Force Sports Control Board and the Subroto Society, I had the honour of conducting the Golden Jubilee edition of the Subroto Cup in 2009, and the privilege of inviting his only son, Sanjiv, to give away the prizes along with the then Chief of Air Staff, Air Chief Marshal P.V. Naik.

It was an emotional moment for all of us because of what it signified.

And a fitting tribute to a true legend.

Which brings us to yet another IAF legend and highly decorated war hero—Wing Commander K.K. 'Jumbo'

Mazumdar—the only Indian to win two Distinguished Flying Crosses (DFC) in World War II, one each in Burma and Europe.

After completion of his initial flying training at Cranwell, Jumbo joined No. 1 Squadron, Royal Indian Air Force. He was a natural in the skies and was soon promoted to Flight Commander of 'C' Flight. In June 1941, he took over command of the squadron at Miranshah in present-day Pakistan.

In early 1942, Burma fell to the Imperial Japanese Army and No.1 Squadron was moved to Burma, arriving there on 31 January. The very next day, the airfield was heavily bombed by the Japanese, but No. 1 Squadron escaped damage, having camouflaged their aircraft well. But Jumbo, roused and combative as always, wanted to hit back immediately, even though the Westland Lysanders that the squadron flew, were primarily reconnaissance aircraft, and their employment in offensive bombing or ground attack missions was unheard of.

Undaunted by such minor details, Jumbo flew out solo, two 250-pound bombs strapped under his wings, escorted by two Brewster F2A Buffaloes from No. 67 Squadron of the RAF, staffed by personnel from New Zealand.

Flying out at treetop level to avoid detection, he attacked the enemy airfield, achieving complete surprise and causing extensive damage, dropping his bombs with unerring accuracy on an aircraft hangar and destroying the aircraft parked inside.

The next day, No. 1 Squadron hit the Japanese airfield again, this time attacking with a full formation of Lysanders led by the Commanding Officer (CO), damaging aircraft, hangars and communication equipment. And this continued on a regular basis till their withdrawal from Burma. In the normal course, the slow, lumbering Lysanders would have been no match for the Jap Zeros and Oscars, but the courage and skill of the Indian pilots ensured that each mission was a success. The credit for this, went to a large extent, to their young, dynamic CO.

Their sterling efforts earned the unit a commendation from the Commander-in-Chief of the Allied Forces in India, and won Jumbo the first of his two DFCs, becoming the first Indian Officer to be so decorated during World War II.

He was soon promoted to Wing Commander, becoming the first Indian to achieve this rank. But in late 1943, itching to see more wartime action, he volunteered to serve on the Western Front and arrived in England early next year. To get back to active operations, Jumbo voluntarily relinquished his acting Wing Commander rank and reverted to his substantive Squadron Leader rank, something almost unheard of in the Forces.

But then, he was always someone who followed his heart.

After converting to the American P-51 Mustangs at 41 OTU (Operational Training Unit), Jumbo joined No. 268 Squadron, RAF, a photo-reconnaissance unit, at RAF Gatwick in early June 1944.

During his operational tour of 100 days till September 20, he was to fly sixty-five tactical photo reconnaissance missions in the Mustang and Hawker Typhoon aircraft.

These included two outstanding low-level sorties, one skimming the bridges of the river Seine, flying through an absolute hailstorm of flak from German anti-aircraft guns on the ground, and another over the Falaise Gap in Normandy, taking photographs of the defensive positions.

He was shot down over enemy lines on one occasion, but successfully managed to avoid the Germans and return to base. This was not a first for Jumbo—he had previously force-landed in the dense jungles of Burma after his engine quit on him, but had somehow managed to walk back to his unit through the jungle. Both wonderful examples of his bravery and quick thinking in extreme adversity.

His photographs were later used by 'Monty', Field Marshal Bernard Law Montgomery, in the famous Battle of the Falaise pocket. The Seine missions were specifically mentioned in the citation for his second DFC in January 1945, a rare honour given to very few pilots in World War II.

It made him the most decorated Indian pilot of that war.

He was already quite a celebrity by then; his portrait had been painted by the famous British artist William Dring of the Royal Academy of Fine Arts as part of his series on World War II pilots and he had been featured in *Life*, acknowledging his superb piloting skills and indomitable courage.

On his return to India after completion of his tour of duty on the Western Front, he was posted as the CO of an Air Display Unit in Lahore. On 17 February 1945, while practising aerobatics for an air show at Walton Airbase, his Hawker Hurricane developed a snag in the dive and stalled, killing him.

He was just thirty-one.

The aircraft that he was flying that fateful day had a history of technical problems, but Jumbo, never one to back down from a challenge, decided to take it on, with tragic results.

He died as he had chosen to live, carefree and daring, taking risks and flying to his heart's content.

He was buried at the Walton cemetery in Lahore, with the headstone bearing these lines 'Go, passers-by and do if you can, as he did, A Man's part in the defence of liberty.'

A true hero and legend, Wing Commander Karun Krishna Mazumdar was one of the pioneers whose stirring wartime exploits carved out a permanent niche for Indian pilots amongst the very best in the world.

A place that they continue to hold proudly.

2

The Bomber That Flew in from an Aircraft Graveyard (1948–1969)

The IAF B-24 Liberators: The Incredible Story of India's First Heavy Bombers

This is a story from long ago.

It is an incredible tale of a newly independent nation and its people, who had lived a large part of their lives under foreign rule, and their idealistic desire to build their own destiny. Of a generation that had seen two World Wars and an Air Force that had flown under a foreign flag. Of men of great courage and grit, who endeavoured and succeeded against all odds, to give their fledgling nation a sorely needed Heavy Bomber when it could not afford one from the world markets. Instead, they rummaged through an aircraft graveyard and came up with the remains of an iconic World War II aircraft that the world had junked and forgotten. And in the stuff of fairy tales, they built two operational squadrons from those ghost aircraft and flew them successfully for the next twenty years.

Their names and incredible achievements are now long forgotten, unknown to most today. And therein lies a tale that bears retelling, time and again.

Early Days

The story begins at the close of World War II in 1945. The world had finally come to the end of one of the longest and bloodiest wars in human history, fought across multiple theatres around the globe. A war that wiped out an entire generation and left those that survived, weary and anxious to go home, unbelieving of their good fortune.

In the Eastern CBI (China Burma India) Theatre, the RAF and the US Army Air Force's (USAAF) Tenth Air Force and 308th Bombardment (Heavy) Group, operated the iconic B-24 Liberator Bombers and C-87 Liberator Express Transports, out of a network of small airfields in east and north-east India, including Ranchi in erstwhile undivided Bihar and Panagarh, Dum Dum, Kalaikunda (Kharagpur), and Salua in undivided Bengal, and mainly from Chabua, Kumbhigram, and Jorhat in Assam.

They attacked Japanese military targets in China, Myanmar and Malaysia and flew numerous hazardous bombing and logistics support missions over the Himalayas at heights above 25,000 feet, to south-eastern China and Burma.

They also moved men and material and euphemistically called it, 'Flying the Hump' (i.e. flying over the Himalayas).

After the War ended in August 1945 with the Japanese surrender, the 308th remained in India in support of US Forces in the CBI, finally sailing out for home in December 1945, leaving their B-24s behind for the RAF to dispose.

Many of the pilots who flew the B-24s were wary of them, since they were difficult to handle at the best of times and had a poor, low speed performance, earning them some uncomplimentary nicknames, such as the Flying Boxcar and the Flying Coffin.

After the war, it was not financially viable to fly these aircraft back to their home countries and so nearly 100 B-24 Liberators were abandoned as junk at Chakeri airfield in Kanpur. Most of these were former RAF aircraft, which the USAAF had provided under a Lend-Lease Agreement that stipulated that they should not fall into unauthorized hands after the war.

Although some of the abandoned Liberators had originally belonged to the USAAF and others to the Royal Canadian Air Force (RCAF), their final disposal, as the huge Allied military establishment in India gradually shut down after the war, was the responsibility of the RAF.

The RAF took up the onerous task of disabling the iconic aircraft so that they could never be flown again. Not so long ago it had been their job to keep them flying at all costs. And to be fair to them, they did their best to damage the aircraft and make them unusable. Bulldozers and trucks were rammed into fuselages and cockpit windows, instruments were smashed, and sand poured into the engines. But in their anxiety and haste to go home after a long, wearying war, they just may have cut a few corners here and there, and not all aircraft were completely written off.

And so, they lay, in that forgotten aircraft graveyard at Chakeri, broken, forlorn and abandoned; vegetation growing over a once-proud aircraft that had struck terror in the hearts of the enemy in its heyday.

No one in their wildest dreams would have ever imagined that there would be an attempt to fly those wrecks again.

But they reckoned without the resourcefulness, need, and sheer determination of Indians.

The Incredible Salvage of a Forgotten Icon

Two years later, on 20 October 1947, months after the nation became Independent, the so-called Pukhtoon tribal raiders, invaded Kashmir and unleashed a reign of terror and killings in the pristine Kashmir valley, burning and looting their way right up to the gates of Srinagar. A desperate Maharaja Hari Singh of Kashmir appealed to the Government of India for help and the Indian Air Force swung into action. Its Douglas DC-3 Dakotas, fondly called Daks, flew round the clock, airlifting sorely needed army troops and ordnance into the state overnight. IAF

Spitfires and Tempests, and even Harvards, flew sorties in support of ground forces, until gradually, inch by inch, the raiders were beaten back.

In those desperate days, there was an urgent need to relentlessly bomb the intruders to break their morale and cut off supply lines. But the IAF had no heavy bombers, other than the British Hawker Tempest, a fighter-bomber that could barely carry two 1000-pound bombs under the wings. Desperate times called for desperate measures and Air Commodore Mehar Singh, the Air Officer Commanding of the Operations Group in Kashmir, turned to the Dakotas, and although primarily a cargo and troop movement aircraft, he used them as bombers. Bombs were loaded into the fuselage (body) of the Daks and literally rolled off the aircraft through the side cargo door. Without any aiming guidance mechanism, the crew had to literally guess when to push their bombs out!

The fighting in Kashmir finally ended on 31 December 1948 with a UN-brokered ceasefire. To the new country and its young Air Force, it had brought the realization that they were in desperate need of a heavy bomber. But the country's finances of the time just couldn't support such an ambition.

It was then that Air HQs thought of the aircraft graveyard at Chakeri and sent out a team of engineers and technicians to see if something could be salvaged from the still-imposing wrecks of the nearly 100 B-24 Liberators rotting away for nearly three years.

When I try to imagine what the place would have looked like to the team on arrival, it reminds me of the time when I was posted at Air Force Station, Barrackpore as a young Flight Lieutenant. My office was located in a large, overgrown hangar behind the Station Headquarters and the open spaces around it were home to old Caribou and Otter aircraft, phased out by the IAF and abandoned there till a 'global tender' was completed for their sale. When that finally happened, I doubt any of them were actually flown out, given the state they were in, and were most likely, simply dismantled and cannibalized for spares.

Or just sold for scrap.

I would sometimes climb into the cockpits of the abandoned aircraft and look at the banks of long-dead dials on the instrument panels. It was an eerie feeling, thinking of the people who had sat there before me, engines running, needles and throttle quivering, engine noise rising to a deafening crescendo through the open cockpit windows. It almost felt as if those men had left a part of their selves behind in those proud, now quiet, forgotten old aircraft.

Their tail numbers gave away a wealth of information for each, of hours spent in the air and missions flown under enemy fire, with bullets striking the fuselage. Of tense sorties in bad weather and dealing with in-flight instrument emergencies, or even worse, engine malfunction. The Otters specially, played a stellar role in the 1962 war with China.

Information now buried in some long-forgotten pilot's logbook somewhere, documenting some of the most exciting, adrenaline pumping, vibrantly-alive hours in the life of its owner. For those extraordinary young men who once sat in these cockpits, flying was a passion that they lived for, a calling, rather than simply a profession or job.

And once you have that, it never leaves you, keeping you forever young and excited, regardless of chronological age, even if it is to simply relive those times again in your mind.

And that is how those abandoned, hulking old ghosts at the Chakeri aircraft graveyard would have looked and felt like, to the first teams of IAF technicians when they came down to examine them.

After they had completed their surveys and due diligence, the teams reported back to Air HQ with the finding that it might just be possible to make some of those forgotten old aircraft flyable again, by cannibalizing parts from others.

By then, production of Liberators had ceased in the US in the post-World War II era, and no aircraft company was able or willing to supply spares, or even flying manuals. The Kanpur Air Force Base had no facilities to service these aircraft and the only way to carry out the massive overhauls necessary to get them flying again, was to somehow move them back to the Hindustan Aeronautics Limited (HAL) workshops in faraway Bangalore.

Since the railways did not have the wherewithal to transport these mammoth, 67 ft long, 110 ft wide, 29,000 kg 'heavies' to Bangalore, the only option available was to patch them up as best as possible, and somehow enable an initial, near-suicidal flight to Bangalore, literally on 'a Wing and a Prayer'.

Chances were that only around 10 per cent of them would make it there safely, the rest perishing midway, killing the pilots who dared to undertake those ill-advised flights.

Qualified American B-24 pilots were contacted, but the fees that they quoted for each hazardous journey, was unaffordable for the new nation.

This brought HAL, then a large aircraft servicing organisation into the picture. Hindustan Aircraft had been set up in December 1940 to provide maintenance support to the Royal Air Force during World War II and had worked extensively on maintaining and overhauling Allied aircraft and assembling fighters and bombers of US origin. This had given them the opportunity to work on another iconic World War II aircraft, the Douglas DC3 Dakota. The DAKs had the same Pratt & Whitney R-1830 radial engines as the Liberators. Post-Independence, HAL was officially handed over to the Indian government and Hindustan Aircraft became Hindustan Aeronautics Limited.

When asked to undertake the possible salvage of the junked Liberators, HAL readily agreed.

At this stage, the then Chief Test Pilot (CTP) of HAL, Capt. Jamshed (Jimmy) Kaikobad Munshi and a team of engineers under the leadership of Mr Yellappa, stepped up and took charge of the operation. They undertook the initial on-site repairs to the abandoned aircraft, necessary to make them flyable for the hazardous journey to Bangalore. Broken cockpit windows and windshields were patched up and some basic on-site maintenance was carried out on the engines in an effort to get some of those massive four-engine aircraft to start up. Once that happened, the first ground runs were conducted by Yellappa's men, and the silent hulks slowly came back to life again.

Back from the dead, so to say.

Jamshed 'Jimmy' Munshi—The Man Who Flew Out Ghosts from a Graveyard

The intrepid Jimmy Munshi was ready to fly out these 'ghost ships' to Bangalore, on what could essentially turn out to be suicide missions. Adding to the overall degree of difficulty was the fact that he had never flown Liberators or any other four-engine aircraft before, although he did have extensive flying experience on the twin engine DC-3 Dakota with its similar Pratt and Whitney engines.

Jimmy and his younger brother Rustam had grown up at Hyderabad, a cradle for much of the early Indian flying. Their father, Nawab Kaikobad Jang Bahadur, had gifted them a Tiger Moth aircraft of their own, and Jimmy and Rustam often flew to Bombay in their prized possession, to buy aviation fuel. They soon built up the necessary hours and expertise to become commercial pilots, and Jimmy joined Deccan Airways and flew DC-3s for many years for them.

Unfortunately, Rustam, who became a fighter pilot in World War II, failed to pull out of a low-level dive in a Hurricane Mk II and was killed in a crash on 27 January

1944 at Rajkharswan, thirty miles west of Ranchi town in modern-day Jharkhand. He was a young, twenty-six-year-old Flying Officer of the Royal Indian Air Force at the time.

It is said that the then Minister for Commerce, Mr Shyama Prasad Mukherjee, persuaded Jimmy to give up his airline job and join HAL as its first Chief Test Pilot. Apart from his usual job of flight-testing various types of aircraft after overhaul, Jimmy now also had the task of ferrying back the roughly patched up B-24s, from Kanpur to Bangalore.

And he relished the daunting challenge immensely. His first objective was to recreate a useable flight manual for the aircraft. In the normal course, each aircraft would have carried its own copy of the flight manual. But preservation of the manuals had obviously not been a priority for the RAF, when the aircraft were being wrecked and abandoned at Kanpur. And so, Jimmy scoured through silent cockpits and sometimes found a few pages here, and a few pages there, as he painstakingly pieced together an entire flight manual for the B-24s. At take-off, this would be handed over to the Flight Engineer to 'rattle out' the checklists for each stage of flight.

The story goes that things were so uncertain that an equally intrepid Mrs Munshi refused to let her husband fly those missions alone and insisted on accompanying him in the cockpit, in the co-pilot's seat. She wore a fur coat to cope with the cold, draughty, unpressurized, unheated cockpits of the Liberators.

On a typical day, Jimmy would start up his engines early, with battery support from the ground crew, open power on the four engines, and if everything functioned normally, taxi around the tarmac to check that the engines were delivering full power, and the brakes were serviceable. With minimum fuss, he would then turn into the wind and take off from Chakeri, en route to Bangalore, 1500 km away, flying with wheels down, throughout the journey. He did this because the hydraulic system that operated the wheels was unreliable and there was no guarantee that they would come down again, once retracted after take-off!

Miraculously, only one flight is known to have had an in-flight emergency, when a small fire erupted mid-air, behind the pilot's seat. Fortunately, flasks of coffee were at hand and were quickly poured onto the fire, successfully extinguishing it, much to everyone's relief.

So confident was Jimmy about these patched-up aircraft that he even provided a 'lift' to two IAF Flight Cadets who hitched a ride in one of his B-24s, without realizing what they were signing up for! If they were mystified to see Mrs Munshi in her fur coat, in the co-pilot's seat, they hid their surprise well. On that flight as the aircraft taxied out, the front windshield glass suddenly cracked. Undaunted, Jimmy taxied back to dispersal for quick repairs and the engineers stuck some fabric on the glass and declared the aircraft good to go!

So off they went again and flew safely onwards to Bangalore, without further mishap, for the Flight Cadets to commence their careers in the IAF.

And in such day-to-day acts of fantastic courage, repeated many times over, risking his life each time he got airborne, Jimmy Munshi flew out an incredible forty-two Liberators from Kanpur to Bangalore, where a team of HAL technicians waited to undertake a complete overhaul of the iconic aircraft.

It is said that when HAL offered to pay Jimmy 'a handsome amount' per flight for the risk that he was taking, he refused, saying he was simply doing a job for which he was already being paid by HAL. Such was the idealism and nationalistic fervour of the time! The nation owes a debt of gratitude to him and to Mr Yellappa and his men, for attempting the impossible—and making it work.

The Liberators in Service

The rest is history. HAL put together two operational squadrons of B-24 Liberators from the junked aircraft, adding a third later, and incredibly, the IAF had acquired the first heavy bomber on its inventory from an aircraft graveyard.

The first six refurbished B-24s were handed over to No. 5 Squadron, the Tuskers, on 5 November 1948. And in tandem with No. 6 Squadron, the Sea Dragons, the IAF operated these aircraft for the next two decades, till they were finally phased out from service in 1968.

News of the Liberators flying for the IAF soon reached surprised American ears. They were apprehensive that the Indians had clandestinely obtained them from a rogue nation.

To put things in perspective, a USAF team was invited to come down and have a first-hand look for themselves. They arrived in India in 1951 and were amazed at the way the Liberators had been restored. Some American pilots who had flown them earlier went to the extent of saying that these aircraft handled even better than the originals.

Soon afterwards, the RAF offered to send their own pilots and technicians to help the IAF with training and any other support that they might need in the handling of the refurbished aircraft.

Flying the Liberators

And so, the IAF had its own long range, high altitude heavy bombers at last. With an all-up weight of nearly 29,000 kg they went into service with No. 5, 6 and 16 Squadrons and two recovered C-87 aircraft formed the No. 102 Survey Flight. C-87s were modified Liberators used for photo reconnaissance, with the armaments removed. They carried no guns, no bomb bays and no gun turrets and were essentially stripped-down versions of the Bomber. Since they were lighter by about 3000 kg, they were a little faster, although still very slow by modern standards, and were called the 'Liberator Express'.

They could do 180 knots in cruise settings, compared to 160 knots by the Bombers, and climb to altitudes of up to 29,000 feet, equal to the height of Mount Everest. The C-87s were mainly used for survey work, to map uncharted terrain and update old maps.

During the first Republic Day celebration in 1950, a nine-aircraft Liberator formation did a majestic flypast over the then, Kingsway, later called Rajpath, and now Kartavya Path, led by Wing Commander Gohel, CO 6 Squadron. Four years later, in early 1954, the IAF showcased the B-24s again at a public Fire Power Demonstration (FPD) at Tilpat Firing Range near Delhi, to mark the twenty-first anniversary, the 'coming of age' of the IAF. The highlight of the show was a demonstration of the awesome destructive power of 'stick bombing' in which, formations of Liberators dropped 'sticks' of 500-pound bombs in a breathtaking show of the 'carpet-bombing' technique of that era.

During a rehearsal with live bombs on 26 March, eight B-24s dropped thirty-two 500-pound bombs, the sound of which reverberated through the city of Delhi. And while the bombs landed on target, the sound of the explosions and the thunderous roar of the four Turbo Supercharged Pratt and Whitney 1830 Radial engines created such a huge racket that the windows of Parliament House, in direct line with Tilpat, 25 km away, shook and rattled. The honourable MPs came rushing out of Parliament in panic and an infuriated Prime Minister, Pandit Nehru, cancelled the FPD forthwith, only to relent subsequently on the counsel of his scientific adviser.

The unprecedented crowds that turned up to watch the FPD brought traffic in Delhi to a standstill in one of its biggest traffic jams ever.

The previous year in May 1953, one of the C-87 Photo Recce Liberator Express aircraft, had famously photographed Mount Everest when Sir Edmund Hillary and Tenzing Norgay climbed the iconic peak for the first time in history. The aircraft had taken off with a full load of eager photographers using oxygen masks, keen to film the iconic conquest live, but had to be called back at the last moment, following apprehensions that the loud engine noise could trigger an avalanche on the mountain, putting the climbers at risk . . .

Pictures of Mount Everest were taken on a subsequent flight, once the expedition was down, and the stunning visuals amazed the world.

With the advent of the jet era, No. 5 and 16 Squadrons changed over to the much faster British Canberra bombers. But 6 Squadron continued flying the Liberators in a maritime reconnaissance role, including a number of patrols in the 1965 Indo-Pak War. This was one of the most vital roles undertaken by the B-24s: to keep our shipping lanes free of enemy interference and deny use to hostile forces. They also participated in the liberation of Goa, Daman and Diu in December 1961, dropping surrender leaflets and flying reconnaissance missions along the sea-lanes linking Diu and Daman.

Conversations with the Magnificent Men in their Iconic Flying Machines

I was lucky to speak to Wing Commander Balu Narayanan of 6 Squadron, long retired and now in his eighties, who was with the squadron way back in 1966. By the time he joined the Sea Dragons at Poona, Liberators were on the verge of being phased out by the IAF, and there were only five aircraft left, four Bombers and one Liberator Express.

He fondly remembers the powerful Turbo Supercharged Pratt and Whitney engines, with their pressurized magnetos that ensured delivery of a steady electrical current to the spark plugs, even at high altitudes. An external battery support was needed to start up the first engine and the twenty-four-hour duty crew unit available at all times in the Air Traffic Control tower would wheel out their starting trollies for this . . .

'The Liberator was a patched-up wonder that had the flying characteristics of a duck and floating characteristics of a brick. The Turbo Supercharged engines at take-off power were an absolute banshee wail and ear defenders were a must,' he reminisces.

Liberators were seldom, if ever, used in an actual bombing role by the IAF, he says, although they did rehearse bomb runs with practice 25 pounders. They were not used for the bombing role mainly because once jet aircraft arrived on the scene in the 1950s, the World War II vintage, propeller-driven aircraft became obsolete, since they were much too slow.

The only way they could have gotten away safely after a raid, was to go in really low over a target, release their bombs and make a quick getaway at equally low level. But their slow cruising speeds meant that the fighters would eventually catch up with them anyway and then the slow, lumbering aircraft from another era would be 'dead ducks'.

So the English Electric Canberra jets gradually took over the bombing role for the IAF and carried it out with distinction, both in the 1965 and 1971 wars with Pakistan. Canberras were flying for the IAF in an operational role till as late as 1999, during the Kargil operations.

The Liberators however, continued to be extensively used for Maritime Reconnaissance and Air Sea Search and Rescue (ASSR) patrols, skimming the waves at heights ranging between 100 feet and 1500 feet, calling for some really strong nerves and sturdy flying by the pilots. On one such mission, he recalls they had a dire emergency immediately on take-off, when numbers one, two and three engines went into a rogue propeller configuration. With only number four engine delivering normal power, they were barely 20 feet above ground, 1 mile after take-off and at 60 feet after three miles, still below the tops of surrounding towers. The pilot, a young Flight Lieutenant, kept his cool and somehow turned the aircraft away from populated areas and managed to land back safely after carrying out a heart-stopping circuit over the airfield at 150 feet above ground level.

Which reminds me of a story by World War II pilot Ernest K. Gann in his book, *Fate is the Hunter*, where he takes off from Agra airfield, on a sweltering day, in a grossly overloaded C-87 Liberator Express. The aircraft simply refuses to gain height and he soon realizes that he is heading straight towards the minarets of the Taj Mahal and looks certain to hit them. He eventually manages to clear them by inches after a desperate, last-minute, use of full flaps to gain a crucial 100 feet, before quickly retracting them again to pick up airspeed and prevent a stall.

To get back to Balu Sir's first-hand account however, ASSR Missions were usually flown in a pre-designated, pre-fuelled, pre-loaded aircraft that would get airborne within forty minutes of a distress call. This aircraft carried specialized rescue equipment called the Lindholme apparatus in its bomb bay. This was a cylindrical equipment that could inflate the life raft on its own, after being airdropped into the water, and carried one, five or seven-man dinghies with lights, Mae Wests, and other survival essentials.

The Liberators would fly out as first responders to a stricken vessel or survivors in the water, and in one case he remembers they went looking for a single man in the water, swept overboard from a naval vessel. On these missions, they would get down really low over the sea and almost the entire crew of the aircraft, including the gunners and signallers, would be scanning the waters and literally hanging out from their open doors and gun-turret windows, looking for survivors and tiny maritime crafts in distress.

When survivors were located, they would drop the Lindholme apparatus near them, improving their chances of survival manifold, and contact naval ships on joint ASSR duty with them, radioing their exact co-ordinates. The ships would then speed out to the spot in a few hours' time and pick them up.

For their own safety, the Liberator crew carried their own individual 'Sarbe' survival equipment, in case of an emergency 'ditching' in the water during those daring low-level missions. This equipment included individual identifiers with lights and a frequency emitter, also known as a Personal Location Beacon or PLB, that could be picked up on radar, pinpointing their location.

These missions could sometimes go on for anything up to ten hours he recalls, and the Liberators could remain airborne for twelve hours at a stretch with the fuel that they carried in their Davis wings and auxiliary tanks.

The usual standard operating procedure at Pune then, was to get airborne and climb overhead to 6600 feet and orbit for thirty minutes or so. If it was 'All Systems Go' on the aircraft, they would set course for their target area, operating at about 8000 feet, seldom crossing the 12,000 feet mark in their unpressurized aircraft that was 'open to the elements from all sides', including sea water and salt spray.

Inside the aircraft, he says it was noisier than a boiler factory at times. The intercom was usually impossible to decipher in that noise, and many a time when the tail gunner called out the aircraft drift readings to the pilot in the cockpit it appeared as if he was saying that the tail was on fire!

Similar was the case with the VHF Radio Telephone or VHF RT, through which the aircraft communicated with Air Traffic Control and other ground stations like naval ships. It was near impossible to get through at times, from both sides. The Dakota had an almost identical problem with their VHF RT sets and were nearly unreachable from the ATC once they got airborne—till the time they finally came back and landed!

For armament, the B-24s had three sets of standard World War II guns, one in the mid-upper turret behind the pilot, one forward in the nose and the twin machine guns at the rear in the tail turret, loaded with 5-inch Magnum bullets in a 500-cartridge belt.

The aircraft also carried bombs and torpedoes and depth charges on maritime missions.

The ten-man crew included the captain or the skipper as he was called, and the co-pilot, sitting side by side in a 'greenhouse style' cockpit. The navigator plotter sat just behind the captain and the mid-upper turret located behind the cockpit was home to a gunner. The bomb-aimer in a prone, lying down position, was in the bombardier compartment and the nose gunner was up forward in the nose. The flight engineer, radar operator and signaller were all located in the space behind the pilots, and the tail gunner, sometimes called 'Tail-End Charlie', was in the powered, rotating, twin-gun rear turret, located behind the tailplane. During World War II, it was often said that the tail gunner had the most hazardous job on the plane as he sought to hold off attacking fighters on their tail with his twin guns. Many a time, he would be the first one to get hit when the aircraft came under attack from fighters firing at them with their forward guns.

Except for the bomb-aimer and the nose gunner, the others were really cramped for space, and the feel was that of being in a World War II U-Boat or submarine.

A long-retired IAF pilot who flew these machines, adds wistfully:

'I was lucky enough to fly these iconic aircraft and had the most wonderful experience of feeling the entire machine juddering under the power of the four P&W 1830 engines at full power, as I held her on brakes. The view from the gun turrets was unbelievable. The Dakota and the Liberator were truly a man's aeroplanes, the feel was incredibly powerful, and they needed you to be on your toes always. Flying Canberras on operations in a Strategic Photo Recce squadron later, was a much quieter experience compared to these aircraft.'

Disposal and Memories

Eighteen thousand B-24s were built during the War years. Surprisingly, for such a mass-produced bomber that participated in widespread operations in Europe, Africa, China, Burma, and India during World War II, there were hardly any left for display in air museums after the war, and almost none in flying condition, except for the ones with the IAF. When these were finally retired in 1968, many museums around the world put in requests for the iconic flying machines. Today, of the thirteen Liberators left at various air museums, six are from the Kanpur graveyard. Only two are in flying condition, including one from the IAF. All these aircraft were actually flown from Poona in 1968–69, on transcontinental flights to museums in the US, Canada, and UK, a testimony to the skills of the IAF engineers who maintained them and kept them flying.

Today, B-24s can still be found at these museums around the world:

1. The Indian Air Force Museum, Palam.
2. The Pima Air Museum, Tucson, Arizona. The aircraft still carries the No. 6 Squadron Sea Dragons Crest on one side and the USAF Star on the other side. It was flown from Air Force Station, Pune to Tucson, as a gift from the Government of India.
3. At the Collings Foundation, USA, which has a still-flying B-24, resurrected from the Kanpur graveyard.
4. At the Flight of Fantasy Air Museum, Orlando, Florida, flown there from Air Force Station, Pune. It is one of four Liberators that was flown out at the time.
5. At the Imperial War Museum in the UK, a gift from the IAF to the RAF.
6. At the IAF Technical College AFTC, which, as the cradle of IAF engineers in the late sixties, very fittingly had a B-24 on display. A part of the ab initio training for engineering cadets in those days included cleaning and polishing the venerable aircraft, as a tribute to the incredible technical excellence that kept it flying in service, way beyond its normal life span.

Another long-retired Wing Commander who flew over 1000 hours on Liberators and was actively involved with these handovers, recounts those times:

'I was associated with handing over of the Liberators to USAF, RAF and RCAF. They had only a radio compass and radar back then and had to be fitted with modern NAVAIDS like the VOR and ILS, before they could be flown out on those long, transcontinental flights. I had such a wonderful time handling them, briefing and flying with the visiting aircrew, as they prepared for those long-haul missions.'

My coursemate, Group Captain Anil Karkare, talking about his dad, Late Air Vice Marshal S.R. Karkare, a navigator who flew, in both the 1965 and 1971 wars, proudly adds: 'My dad had flown hundreds of hours in the Liberators. To honour him, one of his friends built an aero-model of a Liberator, complete with the IAF roundels and the exact tail number of one of the aircraft which he actually flew the registration number sourced from dad's old logbooks. We still have the model at home and feel so proud to look at it.'

The B-24 Liberator holds a very special place in Indian aviation history and is a tribute to the ingenuity of the Indian engineers who brought them back from the dead and got them flying again. Thanks to them and the intrepid airmen who flew them, the IAF was the last Air Force to fly these iconic aircraft for a good twenty years after the world had forgotten and abandoned them.

And that is an incredibly proud, never-to-be-forgotten story!

3

The IAF in the 1962 War (1962)

Driving toward Tawang, a small town lost in the wilderness in the high Himalayas of Arunachal Pradesh, is a board, a poignant reminder of a time now long past, that commemorates our valiant heroes. It is a 1962 War memorial, one of many in that area and says, 'when you go home, tell them of us and say, for your tomorrows, we gave our today.'

And standing there, you realize nothing could be truer.

Across Sela Pass, deep in the Tawang Valley, high up at 10,700 feet, lies Fort Jaswant Garh, one of the Army posts renamed after the ill-fated 1962 war with China, to commemorate the bravest of the brave who fought here, in the Battle of Nuranang, more than six decades ago.

Here, we were told the amazing story of nineteen-year-old Rifleman Jaswant Singh Rawat of 4 Garwhal Rifles, who volunteered in the heat of a raging battle with the advancing Chinese Army, on 17 November 1962, to crawl forward under heavy enemy fire with two of his equally gallant mates, Rifleman Gopal Singh Gusain and Lance Naik Trilok Singh Negi, and attack a Chinese machine-gun post with grenades. This would provide much-needed respite from the relentless enemy firing and help their unit to regroup and hold that position.

The three young men had volunteered for the task knowing that it meant certain death for them. And by throwing his grenade successfully, even after a grievous head wound, Rifleman Jaswant Singh Rawat, almost single handedly knocked out the Chinese machine-gun post, inflicted many casualties, and held off the enemy.

It was one of the few successful battles for the Indian Army in that war.

The Army decorated him with a MVC, a Maha Vir Chakra (posthumous), our second highest Gallantry Award and his regiment built a shrine at the spot where he fought his heroic last battle and named it Fort Jaswant Garh. A small detachment of men from his unit are now permanently stationed there and with typical army hospitality, serve hot tea and pakoras to everyone who stops there.

And almost every vehicle travelling up that road stops for a while to pay respects to the young hero. The Army likes to believe that he still 'lives', and local legends have grown around his heroic last battle. His bed is neatly made-up every day and his uniform pressed by an orderly. His shoes are shined and kept neatly under the bed. He has been given periodic promotions over the years and held the rank of a Captain in 1998, when we first went up there. He is even sent on Annual Leave every year with a train ticket duly booked for him. There is a firm belief that no harm can befall anyone who has paid his respects to the 'Baba' (godman), regardless of whether he is going out toward Bum La on the Indo-China border demarcated by the McMahon Line or returning toward Sela and Bomdila.

But in the dark days of the 1962 War, Nuranang was still just a small field outpost with a couple of huts, and it is hard to believe that this serene, breathtakingly beautiful landscape, was the scene of one of the fiercest battles of that war.

Further ahead, towards Bum La at 16,500 feet, close to the McMahon Line, the area around the 'IB Ridge', so called in 1962 because of an abandoned inspection bungalow built on a small flat ridge in the mountains, has now been renamed Joginder Nagar to mark Subedar Joginder Singh's equally glorious last battle fought there sixty-one years ago, when he led a platoon of soldiers of 1 Sikh in a ferocious, 'to the last man, last bullet' stand, as they fought off three successive waves of Chinese attacks, before finally succumbing to the sheer weight of numbers of the enemy and their superior arms and ammunition.

He was honoured with a Param Vir Chakra, the nation's highest Gallantry Award.

These were the men who willingly gave up their todays for our tomorrow and it's a shame that so few of us remember or know about them now.

And there were others, equally gallant . . . and even more unsung . . . who lie forever in these beautiful valleys and unforgiving mountain passes, in tiny war cemeteries dotting the region, their names etched on small commemorative stones. They are hundreds of miles from home, surrounded by the snowbound mountains of the mighty Himalayas, that are lush green and awash with delightful flowers and waterfalls and unexpected, meandering streams on the mountain sides, six months of the year . . . and cold and frigid, and forbiddingly white, the other six months.

Quiet birdsong has now replaced the harsh sounds of battle and the final moans of the wounded and the dying in the killing fields of 1962 . . .

This was the setting of one of the darkest chapters of India's military history—the 1962 War against China—and much of the actual details still remain shrouded in official secrecy, decades after it ended.

Or perhaps, it never really ended, for a lot of people still live with the unresolved questions that continue to haunt them. And some are haunted by an uneasy conscience, though the generation that fought and suffered from the follies of people in high positions, has mostly passed on now . . .

It was a dark and terrible time and every single word in Lata Mangeshkar's iconic 'Aye Mere Watan ke Logon', still rings true . . .

. . . and fuels an anger and frustration that refuses to go away, even now.

Which brings us to the greatest myth ever propagated—that the Indian Air Force was NOT used in the 1962 war.

What that statement actually means is that the IAF was not used in an attacking role. But then, that is also the story in a nutshell, of that terrible war itself. We never attacked the Chinese, only defended badly selected, badly equipped positions, often down to the 'last man and the last bullet' or retreated and fell back in the face of waves of advancing Chinese soldiers. Isolated, brave little pockets of men, with little or no support in terms of reinforcements, arms and ammunition, communication, high-altitude winter clothing, medical stores and other logistical supplies, held out in places till there was nothing left to fight with, except their undying patriotism and valour, and were overrun by the overwhelming numbers of the enemy troops, that just wouldn't stop coming at them, in wave after wave of attacks.

Against all odds, the IAF's transport aircraft fleet and newly formed helicopter units successfully took on the Herculean task of supplying and sustaining the army units at those remote, cut off locations, in a way that any nation would be proud of. They mounted a stupendous, round-the-clock air maintenance flying effort to sustain the front line troops and evacuate casualties to much-needed medical care. The pilots flew their pants off in the most challenging conditions, in bad weather and under enemy fire, completely unmindful of their own safety.

These men were the salt of the earth. And their stories bear re-telling, over and over again.

Differences with China flared up from 1959 onwards, when China built the Aksai Chin Highway and India started establishing forward posts, beginning with those of the Intelligence Bureau and the Assam Rifles in NEFA, the North-East Frontier Agency, as Arunachal Pradesh was called at the time, in areas that had only been periodically patrolled till then. But these small ten or twelve men outposts remained cut off from the mainland, unconnected by any useable roads, and totally dependent for sustenance on supplies dropped from the air.

They were unsustainable in other words.

A 10–12 km march would take a day or more in the harsh, densely forested, undulating, high-altitude terrain, plagued with rain and extreme cold, for eight to nine months of the year. And even though the IAF's transport fleet in the north-east, consisting of propeller-driven, piston engine DC-3 Dakotas, C-119 Fairchild Packets and Otter DHC-3s took up the Air Maintenance supply dropping role for these posts in right earnest, it was an unrealistic task in the absence of motorable roads.

The IAF had been involved with air maintenance operations in NEFA right from 1951, when the Dakotas of No. 11 Squadron first flew in men and material to the forward Assam Rifles posts, many of which had been completely cut off after the 1950 earthquake. Interestingly, the Assam Rifles posts were being supplied and air maintained by the Biju Patnaik-founded Kalinga Airways in the lead up to the 1962 war. and this arrangement continued till well after the war.

The forward army bases such as the ones at Tawang, Walong, and Tsangdhar had been stocked and supplied with men and material by the IAF in the months ahead of the surprise attacks by the Chinese at Namka Chu and Kibithu in the Walong Sector on 20 October 1962. Walong itself was a completely 'air maintained' base because there were no motorable roads and even the mule tracks that existed were so steep and difficult that even yaks and mountain porters refused to take them.

The roadhead ended at Tezu on one side, where the IAF had an Advanced Landing Ground or ALG. But beyond, the area was practically cut-off, barring the small grass strip at Walong, 30 km away. A foot march over this distance would take anything up to four days, so these bases remained completely dependent on the IAF for ingress of troops, logistics supplies, and casualty evacuation. And the IAF did a magnificent job flying in men and material in difficult landing after difficult landing on the tiny grass strips in the middle of nowhere, where only the single engine, propeller driven De Havilland DHC-3 Otters could land and take-off, many a time in marginal weather conditions and under enemy fire.

The Otter, designed by De Havilland Canada, was a rugged, single engine, utility aircraft designed for 'bush flying' in the remote Canadian wilds and as such, eminently suited to the conditions at Walong. It was called the 'One-ton Truck of the Air' and was capable of carrying up to eleven passengers or loads up to an operating weight of 8000 lbs. It could land almost anywhere on flat ground.

In an amazing wartime feat, the entire 11 Infantry Brigade of the army was flown into Walong from Tezu airfield by the Otters of No. 59 Squadron based at Jorhat, who had positioned a forward detachment of two aircraft at Tezu from 28 September 1962 onwards. In all, the Otter pilots flew in a total of 414 tonnes of supplies and 2083 troops into the Walong sector in an amazing 982 hours of flying during the one-month conflict. Their untiring casualty evacuation efforts proved to be a huge morale booster for the army.

And they did all this with just twelve aircraft.

Heavier twin-engine aircraft, such as the Douglas DC-3 Dakotas of No. 49 squadron based at Jorhat, and the C-119 Fairchild Packets of No. 48 Squadron from Guwahati, which needed longer runways, could not land on these tiny strips, but they flew countless supply-dropping sorties over the designated Drop Zones or DZs, tiny ridges or strips of flat land tucked away in the high mountains, amidst narrow valleys and steep ravines with thick tropical forest cover. They were difficult to reach and target specially in bad weather and many parachute loads of supplies were blown away into the ravines by strong valley winds. Some would simply bounce and roll past the extremities of the tiny DZs when faulty parachutes failed to open and vanished forever into the thickly wooded ravines below, where they possibly, still lie, to this day. And sometimes there was not enough manpower available to retrieve the supplies, leaving DZs saturated with unpicked-up loads.

Summer, with its reasonably favourable weather, was the main stocking time for the army at these forward posts. Apart from arms and ammunition, medical stores, building material and machines, tons of atta, dal, rice, spices, flour, tinned food, potatoes, onions and even live goats in cages attached to parachutes, were airdropped at these DZs. Brigadier John Dalvi, Commander of the ill-fated 7 Infantry Brigade that was almost wiped out in the initial attacks at Namka Chu, was to say later in his book, *Himalayan Blunder*, that nearly 30 to 40 per cent of these drops were lost because the parachutes failed to open. This was primarily because of a shortage of supply drop parachutes at the time which necessitated reusing old parachutes picked up from the drop zones and forward posts.

Once the fighting began, the Chinese advance was so rapid that it soon became impossible for these unarmed aircraft to fly over the DZs without being heavily shot at. The newly inducted helicopters of the IAF took huge risks and landed at the forward helipads at altitudes above 16,000 feet, but their load-carrying capacity at that height, as per aircraft specifications, was severely curtailed. And yet, they airlifted hundreds of tonnes of supplies and troops and evacuated casualties, under fire, in a way that marks out their contribution as one of the most glorious chapters in the history of the IAF. Each machine, each pilot on an average, flew three sorties in a day. 110 Helicopter Unit (HU) based at Tezpur airlifted 1,80,000 lbs of supplies, 1700 troops and flew a record 650 hours during the conflict. 105 HU, with just seven helicopters, of which three Bell BH2Cs were shot down by Chinese ground fire, still managed to airlift 14.6 tonnes of supplies, evacuate 135 men and fly 558 hours during the war.

It was a stupendous effort, one that the IAF has every reason to be proud of.

And amidst all this, the Chinese kept coming in a never-ending tidal wave, building motorable roads as they advanced, moving up supplies to their own troops, with ease. If only the air force had been allowed to attack and cut off those supply lines, who knows how this war would have turned out.

But that's only in the realm of speculation now.

From the detailed briefings carried out at Air HQs by Squadron Leader (later Wing Commander) Jaggi Nath, who flew daring photo reconnaissance sorties, deep into Tibet over the Aksai Chin Highway and Sela and Walong in a lone Canberra aircraft, without ever encountering a single Chinese aircraft at any time, it appeared that it was only the Chinese army that was advancing into India with little or no air support. He was able to photograph their vehicles, guns, and troop positions with almost no interference.

'We have the run of the skies' he was to say, repeatedly. But no one was willing to listen in the face of strong beliefs to the contrary held by the high and the mighty. In the view of the Intelligence Bureau, not shared by the IAF, the absence of a proper radar network meant that the Chinese Air Force could strike Indian cities as deep as Calcutta and Agra, if the war escalated to the skies.

Squadron Leader Nath won a Maha Vir Chakra for his brave forays into enemy territory in that war. He was to win a second MVC in the 1971 war, making him one of only two Indians to have ever done so. But the vital intelligence and photographic evidence that he gathered in the course of those early missions over Tibet went largely unutilized in the 1962 war.

The IAF had squadrons of Gnats, Vampires, Toofanis, Mysteres, and Hunters standing by at the time, with fighter pilots strapped into their seats in the cockpits in some cases, waiting for take-off instructions that never came. If the IAF had been used at the time in an offensive role, who knows what might have been?

But that remains one of the biggest ifs, ever.

The transport and helicopter fleets flew tirelessly day and night and the aircrews clocked 200 hours a month or more in October and November, each pilot flying at least three sorties a day, with hardly any rest or sleep, to keep pace with the ever-increasing needs of the Army.

Even the fighter pilots joined in, flying as co-pilots to familiarise themselves with the terrain and give the overworked transport and helicopter pilots a break. And the engineers and maintenance staff worked round the clock, as always, to keep the aircraft flying.

Tawang, the main army staging post for men and material in the eastern Kameng Sector, did not have a runway; only a helipad that was mainly serviced by the newly inducted Russian Mi-4 and American Bell helicopters of the 105 and 110 Helicopter Units.

Heartbreakingly, most of the soldiers fought this high-altitude war in their cotton uniforms of the plains in the extreme high-altitude cold that went down to -20 degrees at times with the wind-chill factor. It was brutal and people died of exposure and high-altitude sickness even before the fighting began.

In the Walong Valley, bad weather and strong winds restricted 'good' flying hours to just three or four in a day, on good-weather days, with strong valley winds making it impossible for the Otters to operate beyond 10 a.m. But the Russian Mi-4s in combination with the Otters and the Dakotas and Packets, somehow met those requirements, flying sortie after sortie in marginal weather, stretching themselves and the aircraft to their limits of endurance, airlifting a total of 200 tonnes of supplies each day.

It was one of the biggest logistical operations ever mounted by an air force at the time.

Apart from the supply dropping, troop ingress and exits, and casualty evacuation, the IAF also constantly flew senior army officers from the newly created IV Corps HQs at Tezpur to the forward posts and high-altitude helipads at Tawang, Lumla, Tsangdhar, and the landing strip at Walong.

Air Commodore M.M. 'Minoo' Engineer (later Air Marshal) was the Air Officer Commanding of the No. 1 (Operational) Group, newly created at Tezpur on 8 October 1962, which was responsible for all air operations in NEFA. His main objective was to enhance and streamline the air effort in support of the army so that all requirements could be met. He himself flew in the first sortie to Tsangdhar at 16,500 feet, as his pilots landed at difficult, high-altitude helipads with unprepared surfaces.

On another occasion he remained at Walong till the last possible moment and flew out only when the landing ground was being heavily shelled by the enemy.

Tawang was perhaps the best-stocked staging post of the army in the entire region, where the 7 Infantry Brigade was initially based. It was only in the last month prior to the war, that the supply dropping missions were diverted from Tawang to Tsangdhar, which was then, just a tiny, makeshift helipad and DZ.

By that time, IAF helicopters of 110 HU had flown in tons of equipment, ammunition and other logistical stores into Tawang. The Logistics Base of Lumpu with its adjacent DZ had been completely stocked by supply drops carried out by Dakotas and Fairchild Packets. These stores were then ferried further to the posts by porters and mules and yaks.

The army's sudden decision to abandon Tawang at the start of the war and fall back to Jang and Dirang meant that much of these stores were simply abandoned, in a colossal waste of material and air effort, as troops suddenly withdrew from the 11,100 feet-high Himalayan town, even before a single shot had been fired in its defence. This town, with its 500-year-old monastery, was where Buddhism had first entered India from Tibet.

In a mass exodus from the town on 22 October 1962, hundreds of panic-stricken men and women including

Buddhist lamas from the monastery, retreated down the road towards Jang, carrying their meagre belongings. Mi-4 Helicopters of 110 HU based at Tezpur flew out 176 women and children to Dirang Dzong, on the other side of the 13,700 feet high Sela Pass. That done, the helicopters returned to drop food packets for the retreating troops and pick up the injured and wounded.

They flew an amazing sixty-two sorties that day!

But this retreat was just the beginning of a story that would be repeated time and again in that terrible, ill-planned, month-long war.

Many army officers were stunned at the initial pullback orders. Given the history of sterling achievements of the Indian Army in World War II, and later in the Kashmir operations of 1948–49, they were certain that the Chinese offensive could be countered and beaten back. The brave and staunch defence at Bumla further reinforced this belief and the thought of being asked to withdraw without a fight, was unthinkable to many of them.

And for the brave men fighting and dying at Bumla, with just the one thought in their minds, 'Enemy Shall not Pass', the decision to abandon Tawang was perhaps the ultimate mockery of their supreme sacrifice.

Earlier, on the morning of 20 October, when the Chinese unexpectedly attacked Indian posts at Namka Chu, Tsangdhar, and Kibithu, contrary to the widely held view at the time, that they would not dare to launch a full-scale attack, a Bell 47G-2 helicopter approached the Tsangdhar helipad amidst heavy shelling, in the heat of a raging battle. The helicopter was a common sight at the time because Tsangdhar was still in the process of being stocked by the Air Force and supply-dropping sorties and visits by senior army officers to oversee the preparations were a regular feature.

But when the helicopter did not take off again within a reasonable time, army officers engaged in the battle sent out patrols to check the helipad. They reported that both the pilot, Squadron Leader Vinod Sehgal, CO 105 Helicopter Unit and his passenger, Major Ram Singh were lying dead of bullet injuries at the helipad. This was the first air force casualty of the 1962 war and a photograph of the 'captured' helicopter was widely used in Chinese propaganda material subsequently.

Interestingly, the General Officer Commanding (GOC) 4 Infantry Division based at Zimithang, Major General Niranjan Prasad was to have flown as a passenger in this very chopper, for a spot assessment of the battle at Tsangdhar. He had reluctantly made way for Major Ram Singh at the last minute, only because a heavy wireless set, and battery, needed to be urgently airlifted there.

Major Ram Singh, a Signals officer, was to set up the communication lines that would re-establish contact with the post.

When the helicopter failed to return, the anxious GOC sent out Squadron Leader A.S. Williams, in another Bell helicopter to rescue the crew of the first helicopter. But as he approached the helipad, his helicopter too, was caught in a barrage of heavy fire from all around the post, and bullets crashed into his cockpit, hitting the instrument panel.

Squadron leader Williams sustained bullet injuries, but somehow managed to turn away sharply and fly back some distance towards Lumpu, before force landing. He was picked up by a Mi-4 helicopter and safely made it back to Zimithang, where he reported that Tsangdhar had been overrun.

A Dakota on a supply dropping mission at Tsangdhar early that morning, had been similarly shot at, and took many hits to the fuselage. Miraculously, it kept flying and landed back at the Guwahati Air Base safely.

Once the fighting began in right earnest, casualties started mounting and troops from the forward posts with grievous bullet and shrapnel injuries often had to be carried to field dressing stations on yaks and mules if available, or on makeshift stretchers fashioned out of blankets, tied to guns. If they survived that painful journey, they were picked up by helicopters which, like angels of mercy, were everywhere, at times even landing in the hills at night by the light of torches, to evacuate the wounded. Many a wounded army man owed his life to the brave helicopter pilots who flew those valiant missions.

Casualties in the Walong sector, who made it back to the airstrip, were evacuated by the Otters, flying round the clock, to air force bases at Tezpur, Jorhat, and Guwahati. They were then flown further from there in Dakotas to Calcutta, Bagdogra, and Agra, if necessary, the crews often landing and taking off at midnight from closed runways, dimly lit by Kerosene Gooseneck Lamps.

After the heroic battle at Nuranang, fought by 4 Garwhal, the Army pulled back its troops further to Sela at 13,700 feet. The Indian Air Force had done a wonderful job airlifting logistics supplies within a very short time to the logistics unit at Senge, just below Sela Pass, flying non-stop. Senge had enough supplies to sustain the brigade at Sela for a good fifteen days. The 105 HU earlier operating at Zimithang in October where they lost three Bell helicopters to Chinese firing, had received two new Alouette helicopters by November, and moved in to support the garrison at Sela and Dirang.

Yet, when the time came, the army was disinclined to engage the Chinese at Sela and preferred to withdraw further to Dirang Dzong and Bomdila. This was yet another waste of the huge air effort that had gone into stocking that position.

And the withdrawal simply continued, from Sela to Dirang, to Bomdila, and down to the plains at Tenga, as each of these posts fell successively, almost without a fight, to the advancing Chinese troops, marching towards the plains. And finally, like the proverbial last straw, came the humiliating order to evacuate Tezpur town. The entire north bank of the Brahmaputra was left to the advancing Chinese.

Indian Air Force transport aircrafts now flew out civilian officers from Tezpur, including the DC and SP and British tea garden managers, some of whom had served in the RAF in World War II, to Guwahati. No one was left in charge, and by the evening of 22 November, Tezpur was a ghost town, with thousands of people travelling in bullock carts and every other conceivable transport, crowding the steamer ghat, trying to cross over to the other side of the river. There were panic-stricken families everywhere, carrying bare minimum belongings with them. Even the inmates of the local prison and mental asylum had been turned loose to find their way out as best as they could.

Pandit Nehru had made his infamous, 'my heart goes out to the people of Assam' speech on All India Radio on 20 November and it was clear that Assam was being abandoned and it was every man for himself. Ironically, unknown to the nation at the time, the Chinese Premier had called the Indian Ambassador in Peking a day earlier and let it be known that China would be calling for a unilateral ceasefire on the midnight of 20 November. This was however, not communicated to Delhi in time.

If it had been, the panic and hopelessness of the civilian exodus from Tezpur and the north bank could have been averted.

Some fighting continued to take place in the hills even after the declaration of the ceasefire. For the helicopter pilots, their role now shifted to searching for, and picking up wounded, demoralized, retreating Indian soldiers. And they went to work in right earnest, picking up many stragglers retreating through Bhutan and East Kameng, flying non-stop in the hills. In one sortie alone, Wing Commander K.K. Saini in his Mi-4, evacuated thirty-seven army personnel including casualties from Walong, when the usual, sanctioned passenger load was between eleven and sixteen at a stretch.

This selfless disregard for personal safety by the IAF pilots was nothing short of heroic, almost bordering on the suicidal at times.

In the western sector in Ladakh, the first Chinese attacks at Daulat Beg Oldie (DBO) near the Karakoram Pass and the Chip Chap and Galwan River valleys coincided with the attack on 7 Infantry Brigade, on 20 October 1962, at the Namka Chu valley and Kibithu in the East. The same day, an AN-12 flown by Squadron Leader Chandan Singh was hit by machine gun fire near DBO airfield.

And with that the Chinese had simultaneously opened up a war on both the Kameng Front in the East and in Ladakh in the West.

As in the east, the IAF had been flying in support of the army, carrying out air maintenance for forward posts in Ladakh from well before the Chinese war. By the time the war came, a few short, semi-prepared Perforated Steel Plate (PSP) based runways had been laid out by the army engineers.

Landing on these short runways at high altitude, in bad weather, with no navigation aids on the ground, called for a very high degree of skill and courage on the part of the pilots. The Fairchild Packets, IL-14s, and the vintage Dakotas operating in this sector, were all piston engine, propeller-driven aircraft, whose usual cruising altitude was between 12,000 feet and 15,000 feet. But to safely negotiate the formidable mountain ranges in between, and land at the high altitude airfields on the other side, they needed to consistently fly at heights ranging between 17,000 feet and 20,000 feet or more.

Some crashes happened in Ladakh because of this, particularly with the C-119 Fairchild Packets which were not designed to operate at such altitudes, but the IAF pressed on regardless, and landings at DBO, the highest airfield in the world at nearly 17,000 feet, became routine after 23 July 1962, when Squadron Leader (later Air Marshal) C.K.M. Raje landed a propeller driven twin engine Fairchild Packet, fitted with an additional jet engine known as the 'Jet Pack', designed by HAL engineers.

The original plan on that day was for Squadron Leader Raje to take an empty aircraft on a test flight to DBO with only the Air Officer Commanding-in-C Western Air Command, Air Vice Marshal E.W. Pinto and the Station Commander, Air Force Station, Srinagar, on board. But when he arrived at the aircraft for his pre-flight checks, he found nearly thirty army personnel in full combat gear, ready and already seated inside. The army refused to take them off since the men were badly needed at DBO and after some initial hesitation, Squadron Leader Raje relented.

And so the test sortie flew to DBO with an unprecedented full load. Rarely, if ever, has this happened in aviation history.

When the Chinese attacks came, soon after midnight on 20 October, Indian Army units in Ladakh were in the process of 'thinning out' or pulling out for the winter. The

Chip Chap river valley posts to the east of DBO were overrun by afternoon, and the garrisons retreated to DBO. Two days later, the Chinese surrounded DBO, and the garrison fell back to Thoise. The same day, the Chushul airfield came under heavy fire.

The war in the western sector largely followed the pattern of the war in the east and small forward posts manned by a platoon or a section of soldiers without any back up, were easily overrun by the Chinese by virtue of their superior numbers and weaponry.

The Fairchild Packets and AN-12s were the main heavy lift aircraft of the IAF in this sector, along with the Mi-4 Helicopters of No. 107 Squadron. Posts like Leh, Kargil, Chushul, and DBO had landing facilities for fixed wing aircraft. Other places had only DZs such as Galwan and Shyok in the north, and the posts near Pangong Lake. Before the war, the Chushul runway had barely averaged one landing a day, but at the peak of the 1962 Operations, the number of sorties to Ladakh, was almost touching fifty to sixty per day. Six to eight AN 12s and Fairchild Packets were landing daily at Chushul at the time, and the semi-prepared PSP-based landing strip frequently became unusable. By the end of the month-long war, close to 100 AN-12s and sixty Packets had landed there, in a massive air effort to help the army, which was heavily dependent on air maintenance for both rations and ammunition.

Entire garrisons were flown in and replaced by these aircraft right under the nose of the Chinese Army. On one such occasion, Squadron Leader S.K. Badhwar and Flight Lieutenant Narayanan were flying a Mi-4 helicopter from 107 HU, bringing out new troops, when the engine suddenly quit, and they had to force land in a riverbed. Surrounded by Chinese troops asking them to surrender, Squadron Leader Badhwar diverted their attention, gesticulating wildly in sign language, while Flight Lieutenant Narayanan somehow managed to get back inside the helicopter and restart the engine. Before the Chinese could realize what was happening, Squadron Leader Badhwar had also scrambled back inside, and the aircraft made a quick getaway.

With the Chinese wanting to prevent supplies from reaching Chushul, they established a number of machine gun posts around the airfield, and aircraft carrying out a circuit for landing would invariably come under heavy fire. This made flights to Chushul, and back, extremely risky.

Under those circumstances, Wing Commander Anderson, commanding No. 44 Squadron, the only AN-12 Squadron at the time, volunteered to take on the responsibility of flying to Chushul on a daily basis, clocking nearly seventy hours in the region, in an amazing show of leadership.

He also flew the missions transporting six AMX-13 tanks to Chushul—an extremely complicated operation that had never been attempted before. Loading the heavy tanks into the aircraft without damaging the ramp and tail section called for tremendous technical planning and precision. But the IAF technicians achieved it successfully with the help of the tank crew, including the driver who drove the tank up the ramp and into the aircraft, with utmost precision.

The arrival of those six tanks made a huge difference to the defence of Chushul and helped the Army to hold on to its position there.

And then there were the beautiful, sleek 'Super Connies', the four-engine Super Constellations transferred from Air India to No. 6 Squadron of the IAF, which flew nearly 1000 hours in support of the army, ferrying-in entire battalions of troops and tons of sandbags and even barbed wire and PSP sheets in yet another Herculean effort.

The Russian Mi-4 helicopters also rose to the occasion magnificently, making the IAF justifiably proud of the stupendous efforts of their newly operational helicopter fleet in both theatres of the 1962 war.

Perhaps the only aspects of that painful war, which brought some comfort to the country, were the magnificent bravery of the soldiers who laid down their lives or were captured, severely wounded but still fighting, and the sterling, and to a large extent, unheralded, efforts of the Indian Air Force, particularly its fledgling helicopter fleet.

So the next time someone says the IAF was not used in the 1962 war, it would be right to set the record straight and tell them that it was, and more!

4

Foes Turned Friends and the High-Flying Enemy (1965)

This is a story of two young pilots, adversaries in wartime, one of whom shot down the other in aerial combat fifty-nine years ago, but were destined to became friends after the war.

And of a high-flying foe who flew into Indian airspace from Pakistan immediately after that war and got away in spite of the best efforts of a young Pilot Officer manning an IAF radar that spotted him and scrambled fighters to intercept him.

And like the two fighter pilots, many years later, the young Radar Controller was destined to encounter his unseen adversary as a friend, in a third country.

The story begins on the evening of 6 September 1965, a few days after the start of the 1965 India-Pakistan war, when the Halwara Air Force Base was raided by a Pakistan

Air Force (PAF) three-aircraft Sabre F-86 formation, led by their ace fighter pilot, Squadron Leader Sarfaraz Rafiqui. At the time of the raid, No. 7 Squadron IAF had two Hunter aircraft piloted by Flying Officer (later Air Marshal) P.S. Pingale and Flying Officer (later Air Marshal) A.R. Ghandhi in the air, flying a protective Combat Air Patrol (CAP) over the airfield, which were quickly guided on to the intruding aircraft by IAF radar.

Both these young pilots in their early twenties had approximately two years of service at the time, and both were shot down that day, but ejected safely and lived to fight another day, going on to win Vir Chakras for their gallantry.

Both would become Air Marshals of the IAF later.

In the dogfight that ensued that afternoon, Flying Officer Pingale, or 'Pingo' as he was fondly called, was shot down first in a surprise attack from point-blank range by Squadron Leader Rafiqui. His aircraft began to 'smoke' and he lost control and ejected. The Hunter had a powerful Martin Baker ejection seat that permitted successful ejection even at near-ground level. But the 'kick' from the rockets that fired the ejection seat 900 feet in the air, facilitating a controlled parachute descent, almost invariably caused a back injury to the pilot, and Pingo was no exception that day.

He spent the next few days in a military hospital, recovering from the back injury, before returning to combat flying a week later.

An amazing act of courage, from a twenty-two-year-old!

His wingman, Flying Officer Ghandhi, was able to shoot down one adversary that day, before being shot down himself, by the two remaining Sabres. He too ejected safely and was later awarded a Vir Chakra for downing the PAF Sabre.

Around this time, Hunters from No. 27 Sqaudron, returning from a raid over enemy territory were directed to the air battle by the Radar Controller. Flight Lieutenant (later Air Marshal) D.N. Rathore shot down one of the two remaining attackers, killing the PAF ace Squadron Leader Rafiqui in a notable victory. The third Sabre limped back across the border and crashed on the other side, with the pilot, Flight Lieutenant Cecil Choudhary, ejecting safely.

Ten days later, on 16 September, Flying Officer Pingale was on a two-minute standby for take-off or 'Standby 2', on the ORP, the Operational Readiness Platform, at Air Force Station, Halwara, along with his Wingman, Flying Officer Farokh Dara Bunsha of No. 20 Squadron who had been deputed to No. 7 Squadron for the duration of the war.

His back was still painful from the previous ejection, and he had just returned from a medical check-up in Delhi a couple of days earlier. The intruders over Halwara that day, were again, two PAF F-86 Sabres, this time led by Squadron Leader M.M. Alam, a vastly experienced PAF pilot with nearly 1300 hours on the aircraft, and his No. 2 Flying Officer M.I. Shaukat, a youngster with just about eighty hours on the Sabre.

When the order to 'scramble, scramble, scramble' suddenly blared over the Tannoy (PA system) at Halwara that day, both pilots sprinted to their aircraft, quickly strapped themselves in and were airborne within two minutes. Over the radio, the young radar controller, Pilot Officer (later Air Marshal) R.C. 'Bill' Mahadik, gave them an initial vector to fly, putting them on a north-westerly course towards Jullundur, and directed them to climb to 20,000 feet at a speed of 0.9 Mach, almost touching the speed of sound.

As ground radar kept them updated on the position of the raiders, Pingo, the formation leader, spotted a single enemy aircraft below them at a lower altitude. He alerted his wingman, Flying Officer 'Bunny' Bunsha on the radio and the two Hunters dived towards the enemy aircraft with an exuberant 'Tally Ho' (Let's Go) call.

Strangely, even as they approached it from the rear, the Sabre continued flying straight and level, seemingly uninterested in any evasive manoeuvring. A wary Pingo, sensing something amiss, rapidly closed in on him, eyes peeled and lined up for a shot.

As he did so, from the corner of his eyes he saw another Sabre on the right, closing in stealthily from behind, jockeying himself into a position to fire. This was the Sabre flown by Flying Officer Shaukat.

Pingo decided to take on this new threat and asked Bunsha to continue the attack on the Sabre ahead, which had obviously acted as a decoy to draw them into combat. Bunsha called out 'Roger' and dived towards Squadron Leader Alam's Sabre.

As Pingo banked steeply to the right to take on Shaukat's aircraft, they passed each other at high speed and in a flash, he had thrown his Hunter into a turn and was on Shaukat's tail before his adversary could react to what was happening.

Taken by surprise, Shaukat frantically pulled his Sabre up into the glare of the sun, hoping to blind his attacker and get away from him, but Pingo was an old hand at this.

As Pingo was to say later, 'we had practiced this manoeuvre many times earlier. You can't keep climbing forever into the sun because at some point your speed will decay and your aircraft will fall out of the sky, so I just had to wait and keep looking at the sun, hoping to pick him up as he came out.'

Sure enough, as Shaukat gradually lost speed in the climb, his Sabre fell out of the blinding glare of the sun. Pingo, waiting precisely for this, immediately opened power and went after him, not giving him any opportunity to recover.

As he lost speed, Shaukat knew his aircraft was in danger of stalling, or losing lift and falling out of the air, and tried to level out to prevent that. This was a fatal error by an inexperienced pilot, and it allowed Pingo to get on to his tail.

He calmly manoeuvred his Hunter into a firing position with the gunsight crosshairs lined up on the Sabre's cockpit. A single burst from his guns then would have sent a lethal salvo of 30 mm cannon shells streaming straight into the cockpit, but for some reason, Pingo hesitated for a split second, thinking, as he was to say later, '*Ye saala mar jayega* [the poor bugger will die].'

And in an amazing act of compassion and kindness towards an enemy pilot in wartime, he eased back a little so that the crosshairs of his gunsight moved from the Sabre's cockpit to the engine section and pressed the firing button at 300 yards. He had time only for a short burst, but it was enough to turn the Sabre into a blazing fireball.

Even as it exploded and burst into flames, Pingo had already thrown his Hunter into a tight turn, hastening to Flying Officer Bunsha's aid, who was fighting an unequal battle against the much more experienced Squadron Leader Alam.

'Bunny' Bunsha was one of the junior most pilots of No. 20 Squadron and had less than two years of service, with just about 250 hours on the Hunter at the time. Alam using all his 1300 hours on the Sabre, manoeuvred himself inside Bunsha's turn and was able to get an easy shot at the Hunter, raking him with his guns.

Pingo had noticed this even as he was firing at Shaukat and immediately turned towards Alam. But it was too late and Alam, who had latched onto Bunsha's tail, continued firing at him. Bunsha, who appeared to have been hit, was unresponsive to Pingo's radio calls.

As he closed in on him, Alam turned towards Pingo.

As the two aircraft came at each other head on, Pingo noticed tiny specks of flame dancing from the gunports of the Sabre, a sure sign that Alam had opened fire from a distance in an attempt to hit him with a lucky shot, or make him turn, which would give him a chance to get on to his tail.

But Pingo, fresh from a gunnery course at ATW, the Armament Training Wing, held his nerve and his fire. He knew it was poor judgement to open fire from such a distance in head-on combat, when chances of hitting your adversary were slim, and he wanted to conserve his ammunition.

Even as the Hunter and the Sabre flashed past each other, Pingo threw his aircraft into a 180-degree turn, pulling it up on a wingtip almost, expecting to see the Sabre doing the same, and coming back at him. Instead, to his surprise, he saw the Sabre breaking off and diving away for home. His blood up, Pingo put his nose down for speed and went after it. The Sabre pilot went into a near vertical dive, going down to treetop level to get away from his pursuer and Pingo, in an effort to get on his tail, almost blacked out as he followed him down in an equally steep dive, experiencing almost '9 to 10 G' or nine to ten times the normal force of gravity on his body in the pull out. At such moments, the blood drains from the brain and flows downwards into the legs and can cause the pilot to blackout or lose consciousness momentarily. This happened to Pingo as well, and to make matters worse, the pain from his back injury was almost unbearable.

As he regained consciousness and somehow levelled out of that screaming dive, his vision gradually returned, and he realized that he had lost the Sabre in the haze and was alone in the sky.

Squadron Leader Alam later claimed that he and Flying Officer Shaukat were attacked by two Hunters and he shot down one of them with his guns, and the second one with a Sidewinder missile after an intense battle, in which the second Hunter tried to 'run away from the fight'. Although unsupported by any proof or evidence, Alam was duly credited with two 'kills' by the PAF for 'downing' the two Hunters, taking his total wartime tally to nine kills. In reality however, only Flying Officer Bunsha's Hunter had been shot down that day.

Alam had earlier made a similarly tall claim of shooting down five Hunters in less than a minute, over the Sargodha Air Base on 7 September. Many of these claims were subsequently discredited.

Pingo turned back to base, satisfied at downing a Sabre and avenging being shot down ten days ago, but devastated at losing his wingman.

He had not seen Bunsha again since he went after Alam and fervently hoped that he had been able to eject in time and was safe, but that unfortunately was not the case. The wreckage of Bunsha's Hunter was later found on the ground, riddled with bullet holes. He had not ejected.

Flying Officer Pingale was awarded a Vir Chakra for shooting down Shaukat's Sabre.

Surprisingly, even though Pingo had seen the enemy aircraft literally exploding in front of him, Shaukat had managed to eject in time, saved by Pingo's generosity in not aiming at his cockpit. He landed safely near Tarn Taran, although he suffered a bullet injury from ground fire, during the slow parachute descent from his burning fighter. He was moved to an army field hospital, where an Indian Army surgeon extracted the bullet, and he spent the rest of the war at an Indian POW (Prisoner of War) camp. Alive and safe only because of the amazing act of kindness of an Indian fighter pilot in the heat of war, when he had him at his mercy who chose to afford him a chance of 'punching out' of his flaming fighter.

Incredibly, the two were to meet some years after the 1971 war. Shaukat's home, East Pakistan, had become Bangladesh by then, and the newly formed Bangladesh Air Force regularly sent its officers for training courses at Indian Air Force training establishments. And so it was, in a strange twist of fate, that former Flying Officers Pingale and Shaukat Ali, mortal adversaries in the 1965 Indo-Pakistan war, met as friends at the Air Force Administrative College, and talked about old times over a cup of coffee.

And Shaukat would have no doubt, taken that opportunity to warmly shake Pingo's hand and say a quiet 'thank you'.

As an erstwhile foe became a lifelong friend.

What goes on in the mind of a fighter pilot as he climbs into the cockpit and straps himself in for a combat mission from which he knows he may not return? Does his training take over and focus his attention on flying the aircraft so that he does not let himself think of anything else? Or does he experience an element of fear and uncertainty?

And when he realizes that he has been hit, does he eject from his doomed aircraft in a reflex, split-second action, or is there a moment of conscious thought and decision-making before that happens?

I had asked Air Marshal Pingale (now in his eighties) these questions and I quote his words:

'[G]oing on an operational mission is what we are trained for, so it's just like any other training sortie. There is no fear, just complete focus on the task at hand. Regarding my own ejection, it was a surprise attack. I was hit from point-blank range. My aircraft went out of control and started smoking. I ejected from the stricken aircraft, just as I had been trained to do. There was no time or need to think.'

I was also lucky to get another angle on that dogfight from the young Radar Controller on the ground who vectored Pingo onto the enemy aircraft that day, giving him the initial headings and altitudes to fly, till he had a 'visual' on them. Pilot Officer R.C. 'Bill' Mahadik, who subsequently went on to become the Head of Administration of the IAF, was on the radarscope, and he says:

on 16 September 1965, while manning the morning shift, we observed two aircraft on our scopes, coming in from Pakistan air space toward the Halwara–Adampur region. They were flying at about 15,000 feet and it seemed to me that they were on a 'seek and probe' mission, to draw out our aircraft for an air battle.

We scrambled two Hunter aircraft flown by Flying Officer Pingale and Flying Officer Bunsha, from Halwara to intercept the threat and the mission was handed over to me for coordinating the 'interception'. I gave them an initial vector in a north-westerly direction and asked them to climb to 20,000 feet since the enemy aircraft (or bandits as they are called) were at 15,000 feet. My aim was to give them the advantage of height and keep an adequate cushion for manoeuvring. Since the noonday sun at 11.30 a.m. was already high enough, I reasoned that spotting our Hunters against it would be difficult for the intruders, who were at a lower altitude.

And that is exactly what happened as our aircraft spotted the Sabres easily from their higher perch and swooped down on the bandits with ease.

The formation leader, Flying Officer Pingale latched on to one Sabre while asking his wingman to take on the other to his left. The air battle lasted for about four to five minutes, although it felt like eons. With both formations trying to outmanoeuvre each other, the dogfight that started at 15,000 feet went down to treetop level, with intense manoeuvring from both formations, jockeying to find an advantageous position to take a shot. We were tracking their heights till they disappeared from our radar scopes at extremely low level during the final phase of the dogfight. There was total radio silence thereafter!

Almost an hour after the aircraft disappeared from radar, our CO broke the news that one Sabre had been shot down and the pilot captured by us.

We lost Flying Officer Bunsha in that skirmish, but he fought bravely till the end and my personal view is that he probably mushed (lost lift) into the ground during the low-level dogfight against a superior aircraft, flown by a highly experienced PAF pilot.

In this air battle, we once again demonstrated that our aircraft and pilots were capable of taking on any adversary, irrespective of their superior aircraft and better weapon systems.'

The invisible, high-flying foe-turned-friend story continues and skips to one fine morning, just after the end of the 1965 War with the young Pilot Officer sitting at his 'scope' in the Ops Room, sipping a leisurely cup of tea with the rest of his team. The radar shift crew headed by him which included, his Sergeant-on-watch Sergeant Ganguly and other assorted technical personnel, were chitchatting over the morning cuppa in the cool air-conditioned environs of their 'Igloo' (as the Radar Ops Room was called), at a forward Indian Air Force base in Punjab.

And then all hell broke loose.

Even as Sergeant Ganguly excitedly yelled, 'Sir, there is a raid approaching Pathankot,' everyone scrambled back to their scopes, adrenaline pumping.

The war had ended just a fortnight ago and the armed forces were still on high alert with a round-the-clock vigil mounted by the Air Defence Radars on the Western Front. Any air activity near the border was viewed as hostile, until proved otherwise. And here was an air raid again, reportedly heading towards Pathankot!

The young Pilot Officer, with a live war time 'interception' under his belt, in which he had successfully vectored and guided IAF fighters on to intruding PAF Sabres resulting in their shooting down, was fired up again by the scent of battle.

He excitedly scoured the banks of radar screens in front of him, in the hope of picking up the elusive blip that would reveal the exact position of the enemy aircraft. But while the primary (surveillance) radar screen obstinately refused to reveal an aircraft blip, the IFF (Identification Friend or Foe) scope was displaying a secondary IFF 'track', which is basically the automated electronic response or 'signature' from an aircraft transponder to an 'interrogation' signal fired from a ground radar.

None of the neighbouring surveillance radars at the adjacent bases, had picked up anything and yet, the IFF track continued moving eastwards along the Himalayan range, north of Pathankot.

Sergeant Ganguly, the Intercept Control Technician, was glued to the height tracking scope and systematically scanning the area around the IFF track. He picked up a faint blip at a whopping altitude of more than 65,000 feet (normal passenger jets usually fly at 35,000 ft), but there was still nothing to be seen on the main surveillance radar. Whoever it was, was flying high—and probably above the radar coverage area, or 'Radar Envelope'!

Following laid-down protocols for unidentified aircraft intruding into Indian airspace, the Pathankot airbase scrambled air defence fighter aircraft to intercept the high-flier, while Surface-to-air missiles were put on 'standby 2'.

By now, there was pandemonium in the peaceful Ops Room and the usually cool 'Igloo' suddenly felt hot as the Sahara, as the CO and other senior officers milled around, trying to unravel the 'Mystery of the Missing Blip'.

And while, the unknown aircraft stubbornly refused to show up on the radar screens, it's IFF 'signature' continued to move forward nonchalantly, heading towards Agra.

The young pilot officer and his sergeant remained glued to their 'hot seats' on the radar scopes as instructions flew thick and fast on how to 'catch' the phantom aircraft. But despite all efforts including the odd optimistic prayer to the almighty, the blip stubbornly refused to 'paint' on their scopes.

And the aircraft continued merrily on its unknown mission.

By now, there was no doubt that the unidentified IFF signature was hostile, as it continued to follow a pattern of systematically flying over various Indian SAM 2 Surface-to-air missile Sites. It was also evident that this was no ordinary aircraft and was flying well above the radar envelope, maintaining that stratospheric altitude to keep itself clear of IAF radar, and any unfriendly weapons or aircraft that might want to bring it down. The only known aircraft in the PAF inventory that could get anywhere close to that massive altitude was the PAF RB-57, which was their version of the English Electric Canberra Bomber. But the RB-57 had a service ceiling (or the maximum height that it could fly at) of 60,000 feet, whereas the mystery aircraft was cruising along at 65,000 feet, which clearly meant that this was not a RB-57

A newly inducted MiG-21, piloted by the Squadron Commander, Wing Commander M.S.D. Wollen, was scrambled from the Chandigarh air base to deal with this threat, with instructions to climb to a height of 21 km (nearly 69,000 feet), and await further guidance.

But by the time he reached that dizzying altitude and requested to be vectored onto the enemy aircraft, even the IFF track had been lost, the mystery aircraft having presumably turned back for home and switched off his radar transponder with the mission, whatever it may have been, done.

So, there was 'no joy' (no contact) on that score either. And meanwhile, the MiG-21 was already low on fuel, having used up most of the 'juice' in its tanks in climbing to that astronomical altitude. Wollen had to be called back to base.

The debris of Surface-to-air missiles fired earlier had been picked up on the ground, triggering celebrations on the supposed downing of yet another enemy aircraft, but these were short-lived as the invisible intruder finally decided to reappear. It descended to 60,000 feet and turned towards Ferozepur on the Indo-Pak border.

And as if to rub salt into the young Radar Controller's wounds, he was received by two PAF aircraft at the border in a hero's welcome and escorted to the hush-hush American U-2 base near Peshawar. It was known that a facility had been established by the USAF in the Peshawar Air Force Station, for a major communications intercept and photo intelligence operation on the USSR, run by the

United States National Security Agency. It was an excellent location for them because of its proximity to Soviet Central Asia and enabled the monitoring of missile test sites, key infrastructure, and communications. The U-2 'spy-in-the-sky' aircraft was allowed to use the Peshawar airport to gain vital photo intelligence in an era before satellites routinely photographed and mapped every inch of the Earth's surface and satellite imagery became a routine thing.

What was subsequently learnt through the grapevine, though never confirmed, was that the phantom aircraft was a U-2 spy plane on a high-altitude reconnaissance and photography mission, possibly to obtain vital operational information on the Russian SAM 2s deployed by India, with the intention of using it for attacking similar SAM 2 sites in Vietnam.

Which they did almost immediately thereafter—but that is another story!

The Lockheed U-2, nicknamed the 'Dragon Lady', is an American single-engine, high altitude jet aircraft operated from the 1950s by the USAF and the Central Intelligence Agency (CIA) for intelligence gathering, surveillance, and photography. It is perhaps the most famous spy plane ever built and can cruise for many hours at altitudes above 70,000 feet (21 km).

But to get back to our 'foes-turned-friends' story, we move forward fifty-three years to 2018.

Life had continued for the protagonists in the IAF. Sergeant Ganguly had retired and settled down at Kolkata; Wing Commander Wollen who flew that abortive high altitude interception sortie, had retired as an Air Marshal and the young, wet-behind-the-ears Radar Controller who narrated this story to me, had gone on to become the much-respected Air Marshal R.C. Mahadik—the air officer in-charge administration of the IAF in later years.

And unbelievably, the invisible U-2, reappeared on his life's radarscope again fifty-three years later, albeit as a friend this time. And instead of the aircraft sneaking in stealthily, the now retired Air Marshal was invited with full ceremonial honours to see it at USAF Beale—the U-2 Base of USAF's Space Command, at the retirement ceremony of his niece. She had been a USAF medical officer who had served with distinction in war-torn Iraq and Afghanistan.

They were accorded VIP treatment with the entire base thrown open for them to visit, including a tour of the Radar Ops Room, which mounts surveillance of outer space. He was witness to a couple of specially flown U-2 sorties, to enable him to appreciate how the aircraft was handled by controllers, particularly during the crucial take-off and landing phases.

Information that may well have come in handy for that young Radar Controller from long ago, who had so valiantly tried to track down an elusive unknown highflying foe — and had done his best to have it shot down over Indian airspace.

It would have probably become another Gary Powers story if he had. The American U-2 pilot who was shot down by a Soviet Surface-to-air missile while on a high-altitude spy mission over Russia in 1960 and captured by the Soviets. He was sentenced to seven years of hard labour in a Soviet jail, only to be released later in exchange for a Russian intelligence officer captured by the US at the height of the Cold War.

And like the elusive U-2 in our story, the single-seat jet flown by Powers, had also taken off from Peshawar that day.

5

Hitting Sargodha and the Search for Flight Lieutenant Tapan Chaudhuri (1965)

Flight Lieutenant Tapan Chaudhuri impatiently glanced up at the pre-dawn sky for the umpteenth time. Along with a few fellow fighter pilots from the Battle Axes, No. 7 Squadron IAF, he had spent the greater part of the night at the departure lounge of Palam airport, restlessly waiting for his early morning Aeroflot flight to Moscow to be announced.

A young IAF pilot flying Hunters, the British single-engine fighter jets, he was excited at the prospect of travelling to Lugoya Air Base in Kazakhstan (then a part of the erstwhile USSR), to fly a new state-of-the-art supersonic jetfighter, the MiG-21, then still in the process of being acquired by the IAF.

The entire group of young fighter pilots could hardly wait to be on their way.

They sat up expectantly as the public address system suddenly crackled to life, hoping to hear their departure announced. Instead, it was an announcement for their group to report urgently to the airport information desk.

There they were quietly told to report back immediately to Air Force Station, Halwara, near Ludhiana, in Punjab.

The country needed them, and they would not be travelling to the USSR at this time.

War clouds were gathering by the middle of 1965 and the IAF had taken a decision to urgently recall these pilots to active duty with their respective squadrons, putting their Mig-21 training conversion course in the USSR, on hold.

Called back by destiny as it were, for twenty-nine-year-old Tapan Chaudhuri, 'Chau' to his mates in the air force, he would never have the chance again.

Of late, I had been trying to find out about the truncated IAF career and untimely death of Flight Lieutenant Tapan Kumar Chaudhuri, a distant cousin, who flew Hunters in the 1965 Indo-War.

I had never actually met him and indeed, had not even heard of him, till recently. But I would have probably called him Tapanda, if I had.

As so often happens, down the generations, our families had lost touch and I was not even aware of his having served in the IAF till recently, when I was told about him by a cousin sister. She knew him well from her school days, growing up in the sixties, at the Ambala military cantonment, where her dad (my dad's elder brother), then a Major in the army, was posted.

'Tapan dada' as she called him, was based at the Air Force Station nearby, and would often come home to meet them on weekends and stay for meals. She remembers him saying he was tired of the 'runway grass cutting-*wali* palak *ki sabji*' that was so often served in air force messes.

Amazingly, thirty years later we would be calling the familiar, greenish semi-liquid substance that often appeared on our mess dining tables, by the same name!

The recipe had probably remained unchanged over the years.

She sent me an old black and white photograph of him, taken just before his squadron moved on detachment to Halwara for the war. He looked so young and handsome in his flying overalls with the No. 7 Squadron crest; maps spilling out from the knee pockets, flying helmet casually tucked under the crook of an arm, a devil-may-care grin on his face, all set to leave on another operational sortie.

And it reminded me of a BBC documentary called, *They Shall Not Grow Old*, on the young British soldiers leaving for the Front in the World War I, many of whom did not return, and remained forever young in the memories of those who knew them.

Tapanda had flown successful combat missions in the early days of the 1965 war and was part of one of the first waves of the fabled pre-dawn IAF strikes on the heavily defended Sargodha airfield complex, on the morning of 7 September 1965.

He flew through an absolute hail of enemy gunfire that day and came back home safely.

Nine days later, he wouldn't be so lucky.

I doubt if there is a more daunting challenge for an air warrior than to climb into the cockpit of a fighter aircraft and take off in formation with his squadron mates, one after the other at intervals of a few seconds each, on a wartime mission to bomb and destroy a well-defended airbase, deep inside enemy territory.

A mission from which, some of them would not return.

Only those who have experienced it would know firsthand, the sheer courage and determination that is needed at such times, even when it is their primary reason for existence, their raison d'être, and the job that they had been trained for.

My sister was convinced that he had been shot down by anti-aircraft gunfire on a subsequent mission, having read about it in the newspapers at the time.

I wasn't so sure.

There were reports of a bird hit on take-off, when he was scrambled from Halwara on 15 September, to intercept a formation of incoming PAF F-86 Sabres, and I wanted to know exactly what had happened on that day, when he perished, at a mere twenty-nine years of age.

Information available on the Internet, suggested his parachute got blown back into the burning wreckage of his aircraft after a successful ejection at low level, which was a frightening prospect to consider.

When I contacted the IAF, they did not seem very sure either, the incident having taken place fifty-nine years ago.

Although they were reasonably certain that it was a bird hit on take-off.

I also wanted to know more about the fabled 'in waves' raids of 7 September 1965 on Sargodha, that he took part in.

Hitting Sargodha

The PAF had carried out pre-emptive strikes on IAF airbases at Pathankot, Adampur, and Halwara on the night of 6 September 1965 and in a show of strength, the IAF retaliated massively the next day, attacking the premier PAF base at Sargodha in waves, throughout the day. This was reminiscent of the deadly waves of Luftwaffe raids on London in the Battle of Britain, twenty-five years earlier, in World War II.

Although the PAF raid on the Adampur Air Base had been aborted in the face of IAF combat air patrols guarding the airfield, the other strike formations had gotten through to Halwara and Pathankot, causing damage to aircraft on the ground, particularly at Pathankot.

More such raids would take place in the eastern sector at Air Force Station, Kalaikunda near Kharagpur, the next day.

The IAF was not going to sit idle and take this lying down and hit back with vengeance the next morning.

The Sargodha complex consisted of four airfields at the time and was home to nearly half of the PAF's aircraft inventory. There was Sargodha (Main) with its satellite airfield, Chhota Sargodha to the west, Wagowal to the north and Bhagtanwala to the east, all situated across the river Chenab, around 300 km from the border. From bases in Punjab, it would take the IAF nearly half-an-hour flying time to get there.

In the first wave of attacks that morning, No. 1 Squadron, The Tigers, commanded by Wing Commander Taneja, flying French Mysteres, was assigned the task of targeting Sargodha (Main). He had planned twelve sorties for this strike, leading the first wave of four aircraft himself, followed by two more waves of another four aircraft each. Two reserve pilots were on standby, in case any of the main aircraft became unavailable for some reason. Squadron Leader A.B. 'Tubby' Devayya was one of them.

Heavy with fuel and bombs, the Mysteres would be flying at the extreme range of their endurance or fuel limit, even with the additional fuel carried in 'drop tanks' that could be jettisoned or dropped after they were exhausted.

Even so, they would have very little left for any combat manoeuvres or for flying alternative routes to avoid enemy gun positions, if necessary.

The Mysteres would therefore, always be at a disadvantage against the more manoeuvrable Sabres defending the PAF airfields.

The first wave of four aircraft took off in darkness at 0500 hours from Air Force Station, Adampur in Punjab that morning, followed by the remaining two waves, with a planned 'TOT' Time-on-Target of 0530 hours Pakistan Standard Time. But right from the start, the mission encountered trouble. The third wave of four aircraft had to abort their sortie after drifting off course. And two aircraft from the second wave developed technical snags and had to turn back and return to base.

So there were only six aircraft left from the twelve planned originally that actually took part in the first strike that morning.

One of the reserve Mysteres, flown by Squadron Leader Devayya, was then ordered to take off as a late replacement. However, by then there were no more serviceable aircraft available in No. 1 Squadron, and he flew a Mystere borrowed from No. 32 Squadron, also based at Adampur.

Wing Commander Taneja led his aircraft at treetop level, flying barely 150–200 feet above ground, to avoid detection by enemy radar, and they achieved complete surprise. Although Sargodha had already launched a defensive CAP of two Sabres and one F-104 Starfighter, the first indication of the IAF's arrival over the base was the unnerving sight of six fully armed Mysteres pulling up to press home their attack at 0538 hours PST.

'The first we knew of the raid was the thunder of rockets and the stuttering of cannons,' Group Captain Zafar Masud, Station Commander Sargodha, was to say later.

The Mysteres dived in through heavy anti-aircraft gunfire, dropped their bombs on the airfield, fired their rockets and made a quick getaway. Several Sabres and Starfighters parked on the tarmac were strafed and hit, and one F104 Starfighter went up in flames.

The Gallant Straggler and a Maha Vir Chakra, twenty-three years on

Just as the six Mysteres were pulling out and turning for home, the reserve Mystere, flown by Squadron Leader Devayya, arrived over a by now wide-awake Sargodha airfield and dived in for his attack. His aircraft, the lone straggler, was the last one over the airfield and the first to be sighted by the PAF fighters that had got airborne earlier. As such, he was at a huge disadvantage, and up against fearful odds right from the beginning.

Flight Lieutenant Amjad Hussain (later Air Vice Marshal), flying a supersonic F-104 Starfighter capable of hitting Mach 2 or twice the speed of sound, and armed with two heat-seeking Sidewinder missiles, went after Devayya, who was flying at the outer fuel limit of his Mystere with little or almost no reserve fuel left for combat manoeuvring.

Squadron Leader Devayya was now left with an unenviable choice. He could either turn back after finishing his bomb run and take on the Starfighter, in which case, even if he survived the dogfight, he would have no fuel left to fly back home. Or he could just carry on flying back towards base after the bomb run, in which case he would be a sitting duck for the much faster, supersonic Starfighter. Predictably, the brave Coorgi chose the first option, that of staying back and fighting, even if it meant running out of fuel over enemy territory.

Using his advantage of height and speed and better firepower, Flight Lieutenant Hussain quickly got behind the Mystere and released his Sidewinders, which Squadron Leader Devayya managed to evade, with great skill. Still on his tail, the frustrated Hussain went in with his 20 mm cannons blazing and saw his shells ripping into the Mystere. Convinced that he had a confirmed 'kill', Hussain peeled off from the dogfight in a climbing turn and went in search of the other IAF aircraft.

But Devayya was not done yet and though he was hit, his aircraft was still flying. He could have attempted even at that stage to fly back home, or abandoned his stricken aircraft, and ejected to safety.

But he did neither and instead, turned and went after the Starfighter. Hussain, noticing the Mystere closing in from behind, thought it was another one of the raiding IAF aircraft and turned around to take it on. He was perhaps a trifle overconfident about the superiority of his own aircraft and soon found himself in trouble against a determined adversary whose blood was up.

After a series of combat manoeuvres, Squadron Leader Devayya had the Starfighter in his gunsights and fired his cannons at the F-104, turning it into a fireball.

Flight Lieutenant Hussain ejected from his flaming Starfighter in a heartbeat and never really knew who had shot him down.

What happened to Squadron Leader Devayya is not exactly known. He may have lost consciousness and succumbed to his injuries mid-air, or lost control of his stricken aircraft and crashed. Perhaps, he attempted a last-minute unsuccessful ejection at low level. No one knows for certain, although reports of his body being found near the wreckage of his aircraft and given a burial by Pakistani villagers indicate that he did not eject.

Flight Lieutenant Hussain survived his ejection and on reaching his own base, claimed one Mystere destroyed (Devayya's). He reported that he had been shot down in combat by a second Mystere.

And that remained the official version of the dogfight for the next two decades. And the saga of Squadron Leader Devavya's incredible last battle remained untold.

The remaining Mysteres flew on, oblivious to the combat that had taken place behind them, and after an uneventful flight landed back safely at Adampur.

Only later it became known that Squadron Leader Devayya had failed to return. He was listed MIA or Missing in Action, and everyone hoped he had ejected in time and been taken POW.

And the story of his exceptional act of bravery remained unknown to the world for more than two decades. He was declared 'Presumed Dead' as is customary in such cases, a year later, in 1966.

Destiny was to play a hand in his tale though, and in 1971, Flight Lieutenant Amjad would fly his Starfighter again in a war against India, and being shot down once again, this time by anti-aircraft gunfire over Amritsar, taken POW.

From his subsequent interrogation at Air HQs, hitherto unknown details of Squadron Leader Devayya's last battle would gradually emerge.

However, things started to fall in place only in 1979 when the dogfight was documented in a book commissioned by the PAF, called, *Battle for Pakistan—The Air War of 1965* by British journalist, John Fricker.

When Group Captain Taneja, by then retired from the IAF, read about Flight Lieutenant Amjad's account of a dogfight with a 'second Mystere' in this book, he knew it was just not possible, because none of the other Mysteres on that mission had directly engaged with a PAF aircraft that morning. He was convinced that this must be Squadron Leader Devayya's Mystere that Amjad was talking about, and took it up immediately with Air HQs, to correct a historical error.

Even so, the issue got looked at with seriousness only in 1987 when Air Commodore Pritam Singh, a former Gnat Pilot who had flown in the 1965 war as a young Flying Officer, then in-charge of the Defence Historical Cell, was researching for the Defence Ministry's 'Official History of the Indo-Pak War, 1965'. His efforts at arriving at the truth finally led to the award of a much-deserved MVC, to Squadron Leader Devayya in 1988, the only one to be awarded to an IAF pilot posthumously.

And so, it was by chance, perhaps a preordained twist of fate in another war, that the true facts of that amazing battle finally came to light, twenty-two years later, and the gallant air warrior was finally recognized and honoured for his exceptional bravery and courage.

But to return to the 7 September raids, while No. 1 Squadron was attacking Sargodha that morning, the other Mystere Squadron based at Adamapur, No. 32 Squadron, was simultaneously hitting the Bhagtanwala airfield with eight aircraft, in the second strike of the day. This raid was led by Squadron Leader M.S. 'Mickey' Jatar, who on arrival over the airfield, saw Sabres lined up on the ORP and dived in for a quick attack on the stationary aircraft, strafing them with cannons and firing rockets at his targets.

One of the Sabres was destroyed on the ground, while another one was damaged. PAF fighters were scrambled, but by the time they took off, the Mysteres had made a clean getaway, winging their way back at treetop level. All eight made it back to base uneventfully. The PAF would later claim that the aircraft that were hit that morning, were dummies, a claim that remains unsupported to this day like many of their other claims, by any real evidence.

But this was only the start of that eventful day and the next raid on Sargodha was planned for 0615 hours by Hunter aircraft from No. 27 Squadron based at Halwara, led by the Squadron Commander, Wing Commander D.S. Jog (later Air Marshal). They had the task of attacking the Chhota Sargodha airfield, forty-five minutes after the first raid by the Mysteres.

And this was the strike that my cousin, Flight Lieutenant Tapan Chaudhuri, flew on that day

Knowing that PAF air defence fighters would be stirred up by the first raid, Wing Commander Jog decided to go in with four Hunters, armed with rockets and bombs in a strike formation, shepherded by two other Hunters in a fighter escort role. Unfortunately, during take-off, one of the escorting Hunters became unserviceable and since it was too late to bring in another aircraft as a replacement, only one Hunter went with the strike formation in the fighter escort role that day.

This Hunter was flown by Flight Lieutenant D.N. Rathore (later Air Marshal), who had just shot down a Sabre the previous evening over Halwara, flown by the Pakistani ace, Squadron Leader Sarfaraz Raffiqui.

Wing Commander Jog was leading the strike mission with Squadron Leader O.N. Kacker, Flight Lieutenant Tapan K. Chaudhuri and Flying Officer Parihar (later Air Vice Marshal) as his wingmen. Pulling up over their target as they arrived at the airfield at treetop level, he noticed Sabres parked on the runway and quickly dived into his bomb run, followed by the other three aircraft.

Flying through an absolute hail of anti-aircraft gunfire, the four aircraft released their bombs and fired their rockets, destroying at least two F-86 Sabres on the tarmac. By this time, a couple of PAF Sabres flying a defensive CAP over the airfield had dived in on them from above.

A Sabre opened fire on Flight Lieutenant Tapan Chaudhuri's Hunter, who carried on with his bomb run undeterred. Flight Lieutenant Rathore, flying as fighter escort, turned towards the Sabre to engage him. The PAF pilot saw him coming and broke off his attack on Chaudhuri, to take on Rathore, and the two aircraft passed each other head-on at high speed, avoiding a mid-air collision by a whisker. Wing Commander Jog in the lead Hunter was also fired upon by the other Sabre but his aircraft too, flew on, seemingly undamaged.

Then, as suddenly as the air battle had started, it was over. The Sabres disappeared and the Hunters found themselves alone in the sky.

Wing Commander Jog was happy to find all four Hunters flying alongside. Flight Lieutenant Rathore had also by then joined up with the main strike formation. However, they noticed at this time that Squadron Leader Kacker's aircraft was losing speed. The others throttled back and reduced speed to maintain formation with him, but it was obvious that his fuel tank had been holed and he was steadily losing fuel.

Soon enough, Squadron Leader Kacker reported that his red, low-fuel warning lights had come on in the cockpit and he would not be making it back over the border.

Gradually his fuel ran out and the engine flamed out. As the Hunter began to lose altitude, Squadron Leader Kacker ejected over enemy territory. The other aircraft of the formation radioed his position to base for a possible rescue effort by helicopters and flew on, because even they were critically low on fuel. They knew Squadron Leader Kacker would probably be taken POW and hoped he would be safe.

By the time the four Hunters landed back at Halwara, they had very little fuel left. Flight Lieutenant Tapan Chaudhuri discovered he'd had a narrow escape that day as his drop tanks had been severely holed in the attack on him by the Sabre. But Lady Luck was on his side that morning and he and his aircraft were able to make it back safely to base.

After the first three strikes of that day, two by the Mysteres and one by Hunters, two aircraft had been lost, one Mystere and one Hunter, and the action was only just beginning to unfold.

As they were approaching base, the four returning aircraft were passed by another five Hunters from No. 7 Squadron, heading out towards Sargodha. Wing Commander Jog was alarmed because he knew these aircraft would fly straight into the enemy Sabres already in the air and the waiting anti-aircraft guns. Heavily loaded with bombs and drop tanks, they would be at a big disadvantage in a dogfight, against the more nimble and manoeuvrable Sabres.

Wing Commander Toric Zachariah, the CO of No. 7 Squadron, was leading this mission and with him were Squadron Leader M.M. Sinha (later Air Marshal) and Squadron Leader A.S. Lamba (later Air Vice Marshal) in the bombing role, with the fighter escort cover being provided by Squadron Leader S.B. Bhagwat and Flying Officer J.S. Brar, in the other two Hunters.

Confirming Wing Commander Jog's worst fears, they ran into the prowling Sabres stirred up by the No. 27 Squadron raid, waiting at an altitude around 3,000 feet higher than the Hunters, who were going in low. Even as the Sabres swooped down upon them, Wing Commander Zachariah instructed the formation to split up and select their own targets for their bomb runs. The strike aircraft quickly released their bombs and turned back for base, returning individually at tree top height.

Meanwhile, the fighter escort detail comprising, Squadron Leader Bhagwat and Flying Officer Brar, had turned into the Sabres and engaged them in a dogfight. Both IAF pilots failed to return that day, and it is presumed that both were shot down, bravely covering the return of their squadron mates.

Both victories were attributed by PAF to Squadron Leader M.M. Alam (later Air Commodore), who made a rather frivolous claim of having shot down five IAF Hunters in a span of thirty seconds over Sargodha that day.

Having lost Squadron Leader Raffiqui—their other war hero credited with three victories in the previous night's raid over Air Force Station, Halwara—PAF was only too happy to credit him with these five 'kills' (quite a few of which were discredited later). It made him an instant Air Ace and war hero, which was good for their propaganda. He was to claim a total of nine victories in the 1965 war and emerged as their top war hero.

The PAF claimed the IAF had lost ten aircraft that day and declared 7 September as 'PAF Day'. But in reality, the loss of these two No. 7 Squadron Hunters brought up the total number of aircraft lost by the IAF that day, to four, after as many strikes.

There was still more to come, however.

The next raid on Sargodha Main came over three hours later, when six Mysteres of No. 1 Squadron came screaming over at 0945 hours. This strike, led by Squadron Leader Sudharshan Handa (later Air Commodore), caused extensive damage. They flew very low, hugging the ground at 50–100 feet, all the way to the target, and bombed the bulk petroleum installation at the airfield, setting it on fire. Handa then strafed three Sabres parked on the ORP with his cannons and destroyed at least one of them.

His wingman, Flight Lieutenant D.M.S. Kahai, was even more successful. His bombs hit the remaining Sabres and a F-104 Starfighter on the ORP. On their third run over the airfield through heavy anti-aircraft gunfire, Flight Lieutenant Kahai noticed two more Sabres and another F-104 on the tarmac, and opened up with his cannons, destroying all three on the ground. Mission accomplished, the Mysteres flew back to base safely, leaving over seven aircraft burning or damaged on the ground at Sargodha.

Once again, they landed with bare minimum fuel in their tanks.

The last sorties of the day were flown at 1540 hours, when two more Mysteres of No. 1 Squadron raided Sargodha yet again. This time, the Mysteres were attacked by Sabres patrolling the skies over the airfield and quickly split up. Flight Lieutenant Babul Guha was shot down by a Sidewinder missile fired by Flight Lieutenant A.H. Malik from his Sabre. He was listed missing and later believed killed.

That finally brought down the curtain on the IAF offensive on Sargodha on that eventful day. Overall, thirty-three aircraft flew in six different strikes that day, losing a total of five IAF aircraft and their pilots, in the process.

PAF, however, claimed ten kills without providing any definitive evidence. And it was reason enough for them to celebrate 7 September as 'PAF Day'.

After this day, the Hunter aircraft from No. 7 Squadron, were primarily engaged in a ground-attack role for the next one week or so, flying missions in support of the army. Not much information is available about these missions other than that they attacked convoys of military vehicles and ammunition trains across the border.

Having learnt the details of the combined raids of 7 September, I was still, however, not very sure about what exactly had happened to my cousin Flight Lieutenant Chaudhuri on 15 September 1965, the day he was killed, although the 'bird hit on take-off' report seemed to be the most likely story.

I tried to locate someone who would have known him personally, and my quest led me to Air Marshal Prakash Pingale, now in his eighties, who had actually flown with him in that war, as a young Flying Officer with two-years of service in No. 7 Squadron.

Not wishing to intrude, I WhatsApped the Air Marshal, asking if had any recollection of the incident that had happened a day before he shot down a PAF F-86 Sabre in a combat sortie, in which his wingman, Flying Officer Feroze Dara Bunsha, was killed by Squadron Leader M.M. Alam.

Nine days earlier, Flying Officer Pingale had himself been shot down in a surprise attack while flying a CAP over Halwara. Hit at point-blank range by a PAF F-86 Sabre flown by the Pakistani ace, Squadron Leader Sarfaraz Rafiqui. The sudden burst sent Flying Officer Pingale's aircraft spinning out of control, but he ejected and landed safely that day.

Unbelievably, he was back to combat flying again a week later, although he still had a back injury from the ejection.

The sheer, incredible split-second courage of it all!

I hoped the octogenarian Air Marshal would see my message and respond to it, even though I was asking him about something that had happened nearly six decades ago. Sure enough, the reply came in within a couple of hours, a wonderfully detailed, warm, personalized message that cleared most of my doubts.

He said that my cousin, Flight Lieutenant Chaudhuri or 'Chau', as he affectionately called him, was already posted in No. 7 Squadron when he joined in 1963. 'Seven' was an elite Squadron those days and Chau was an outstanding pilot who was a member of its nine-aircraft formation aerobatics team, led by Wing Commander Katre, the CO (later Air Chief Marshal).

This team was the precursor to the Thunderbolts, the IAF formation aerobatics team which was constituted under Wing Commander Ben Brar fifteen years later in 1982. Brar was himself a young Flying Officer in No. 7 Squadron at the time and had flown on the formation aerobatics team.

But that is another story.

Air Marshal Pingale said he was very fond of 'Chau', even when the squadron was based at Ambala, before the war, and spent a lot of time in his room in the Officer's Mess, animatedly talking about football and theatre—Chau's primary interests—and listening to him playing the guitar.

During the 1965 war the IAF flew many 'mixed' formations to make up the necessary numbers and even though Chau was originally posted in No. 7 Squadron, he flew some missions with No. 27 Squadron pilots, which was the other Hunter Squadron, then based at Halwara, including that daring pre-dawn attack on Sargodha Airfield.

Even some pilots from No. 20 Squadron, a Hunter Squadron based at Palam those days, were roped in to join the No. 7 and No. 27 Squadron sorties to augment available resources, the Air Marshal reminisced.

Which is probably something not many people are aware of today. And indeed, I have seen Chau being listed in some places as a No. 27 Squadron pilot, which he was not. He was actually from No. 7 Squadron.

Talking about Chau's tragic accident, he said he still remembers that day vividly, having witnessed it from the ground.

Chau suffered a bird hit on take-off from Halwara and in a heroic effort to save the aircraft, decided to turn around and land. On the downwind leg of the Airfield Circuit Pattern, the aircraft caught fire and Chau was told to eject. He however, persisted with his approach, but as the fire spread, he finally jettisoned his canopy and ejected on Base Leg, very close to the airfield. Flying Officer Pingale and their squadron doctor, Flight Lieutenant Agarwal, were the first ones to reach him. He had fallen well clear of the crashed aircraft and did not seem to have sustained any major injuries. But he remembers the doc feeling his pulse and shaking his head. His parachute had probably caught fire in the air, and he had succumbed to his injuries.

He concluded his message saying, 'I must repeat, I was very fond of him and spent a lot of time in his room. He was a bit of a loner, but a gem of a person.'

So, there it was, right from the horse's mouth, so to say, a vivid description of an incident from fifty-nine years ago. And I am so glad that I now know exactly what happened that morning.

It had been fascinating trying to piece together the story of these heroic men and an absolute privilege to have worn the same uniform as them (with a few changes down the years!).

Today, there is a road named after him at Kolkata called 'Flight Lieutenant Tapan Chowdhury Avenue' and an auditorium called 'Tapan Theatre' which still has a full-length photograph of him in air force uniform, displayed at the entrance. When I first heard about it, I wondered why a theatre auditorium would be named after him, till I heard about his passion for the theatre. He had actually acted in a number of plays, before the air force took him away from such things.

And the people who knew him and loved him there, named the auditorium after him.

But strangely, while 'Tapan Theatre' itself is quite popular and well-known in Kolkata, I am not so sure many people know or remember who 'Tapan' was, anymore.

These men were true heroes, the salt of the earth, 'the Few', to quote Winston Churchill, in the true sense of the term, who contributed 'so much' to this country in facilitating its journey to where it stands today. Our freedom flourishes and we live honourably today because of their sacrifices.

And that of their families.

And that is why their stories need to be told—over and over again.

Lest we forget . . .

6

Notes from the War Diary of a Fighter Controller (1971)

Squadron Leader M.L. 'Bounty' Bountra stepped out of a barber shop in bustling Amritsar. It was a chilly winter afternoon on 3 December 1971, when he heard the noise of an aircraft overhead and instinctively looked up. Something was not quite right. A Senior Radar Controller by training, he could easily identify aircraft by their engine sound, and this was not something that he was familiar with. This was not the engine of a Gnat, a Hunter, a MiG-21, a Su-7 or even an AN-12—aircraft that he would normally expect to hear over Amritsar. And as his eyes scanned the afternoon sky, he caught his breath sharply as the unknown aircraft swam into view.

For there were the green-and-white PAF markings, plainly visible, something that he had not seen since the 1965 War! Realization suddenly dawned on him that this was a PAF F-104 Starfighter that had come calling on our side of the fence with distinctly unfriendly intentions!

And as if to confirm his worst suspicions, the aircraft opened up with its guns at unseen targets on the ground.

Talk of war had been in the air for the last few weeks, and here it was, the first unexpected PAF air raid over Amritsar.

The 1971 Indo-Pak war had begun.

The young Squadron Leader broke into a run. They were staying in what the military still calls 'civil area', since no Service Married Quarters were available within the Air Force Station at the time. As the 'No. 2' or second-in-command at his radar unit after the CO, he needed to get back to the Base as quickly as possible.

He rushed home, quickly changed into uniform, said a hurried goodbye to his wife and two small children, and sped off on his scooter at breakneck speed.

And as she stood there at the doorway watching him go, they both knew that there was no guarantee, of when and if, he would return home.

'Bounty', as he was fondly called by his mates, picks up the story at this point. 'In early October 1971, when I was urgently recalled from Annual Leave after just one week at home, I knew war was imminent. Hectic activity was on at the unit and unlike 1965, when a number of aircraft had been destroyed in enemy air raids on the tarmac itself, fortified Blast Pens had been built at different places along the taxi track this time, housing the aircraft, making them difficult targets to hit. From mid-October onwards we were put on twenty-four-hour watch and detachments of MiG-21 and Gnat squadrons were moved in for ORP duties and L-70 anti-aircraft guns equipped with radar-guided aiming devices were deployed by the Army around the Air Force Base.'

Back at the unit, the CO and he carried out a quick assessment of the damage that the Starfighter had caused in the sudden attack. They were pleasantly surprised to find that barring a few stray bullets that had struck the 'Slant Aerial', there appeared to be no major damage, and the radar continued to function normally.

He had been posted to Amritsar in mid-1970 and after the mandatory familiarization period, had taken over as the Sector Operations Officer, SOO, of the unit. They had the Pathankot, Adampur, and Amritsar Airbases under them in the area of responsibility, while the other major radar unit at Barnala, a full-fledged ADDC, or Air Defence Direction Centre, had the Sirsa, Halwara, Ambala, and Chandigarh Airbases under them.

His unit, located just thirty kilometres from the border, had always been a thorn in the flesh for the PAF, with its radar looking deep into enemy territory. PAF attempted to knock it out on at least three separate occasions during that war, each time unsuccessfully, starting with that first surprise raid on 3 December. This was followed by another three to four daylight raids the next day, none of which, again, caused any major damage.

The radar continued to function, much to the frustration of the PAF.

However, they managed to hit the main aerial of the radar at Barnala the next day, putting it out of action for two days at that crucial juncture.

The raids continued right through the long, wearying night of 4 December, when Amritsar was continuously targeted by PAF B-52 heavy bombers, almost at hourly intervals. Pathankot was even worse off, bombed every half an hour. For the IAF, it was a baptism by fire, as they buckled down to yet another full-fledged war against Pakistan, the second in six years.

Fortunately, there was no loss of life or casualties, except for a few shrapnel wounds to personnel sheltering in air raid trenches inside the Air Force Station.

There were no civilian casualties.

MOFs (Mobile Observation Flights) to physically identify and report low flying aircraft that would otherwise be difficult to pick up on radar, were still in the process of being formed, and in an innovative idea, the network of railway stations along the border areas, was requisitioned and pressed into service, with the support of the Railway Divisional HQs at Amritsar, to report overflying aircraft. The railways had been widely targeted by the PAF in the 1965 War and were only too happy to help. Teams of radar controllers went around the railway stations and trained the staff on how to identify and report overflying aircraft. Compass circles of bricks and lime were drawn at each station, to facilitate accurate direction reporting. The railway station reporting network proved to be very effective and gave the IAF added eyes and ears on the ground. The station masters had the responsibility of reporting overflying aircraft, and did a wonderful job, with the station master at Gurdaspur winning a special commendation for wartime services.

This network was essential because in those pre-inertial navigation days, pilots would often pick up a prominent ground landmark such as a railway line or a river, or a main road, and follow it to a destination. Railway lines were particularly useful because they gleamed at night, and were easy to pick up from the air, especially at a time when the surrounding countryside was in total darkness because of blackouts.

The inherent problem with this reporting system, however, was that at night no direction reports were possible on overflying aircraft and the usual reporting would be a very unspecific 'aircraft sound heard'.

It took the radar controllers between two and three nights to establish a pattern to identify possible targets when a particular railway station reported overflying aircraft. These could be military bases in the vicinity, or a city or town they could be heading for. Accordingly, warnings were issued, and the Air Defence Guns alerted, and usually, these calculated guesses proved to be quite accurate

Squadron Leader Bountra continues:

[T]here was no fear, just the thrill and excitement of war, and a strong sense of the job at hand. While the enthusiasm and excitement had to be seen to be believed, the atmosphere generally remained tense and an uncertainty about what might happen next, was always just below the surface.

With bombs exploding and Pakistani aircraft attacking nine to ten times every night on the first few days of the war, accompanied by the rattle of anti-aircraft guns taking them on, there were no quiet moments when one could actually relax and "switch off".

Most of all, there was a tremendous adrenaline rush, as hostile incoming tracks were picked up on the radar scopes, and fighters scrambled from nearby airbases in real time, to intercept them. Once airborne, they would position themselves over pre-designated reporting points, and we would then guide or vector them onto live enemy aircraft, so unlike the practice interceptions of peacetime.

Outgoing strike missions over enemy territory would give us a brief call after take-off, and then maintain complete radio silence, till they crossed over again, back into Indian air space. Since these would normally be low, tree-top level missions, flying at 300–500 ft to avoid detection by enemy radar, we would have no pickup on them on our scopes, and in the interest of security, we were not given any details of these missions.

But they would chart their progress and try to time their returns from across the border, based on the fuel capacities and close monitoring of PAF aircraft radio telephone (RT) conversations with radar and ATC controllers, which could be picked up and listened to, in the Ops Rooms.

Radar controllers would therefore have their hands full, watching and guiding own missions, and monitoring protective CAPs flown over our airfields to deter and intercept enemy aircraft attempting to attack the base. Or staying in touch with the "Sparrow", the single aircraft orbiting above, that often served as an airborne, mobile ATC or radar controller, especially at night. The 'Sparrow' could make radio contact even with low flying, ground-hugging aircraft returning from operational missions because of its height and relay their transmissions to radar and ATC controllers on the ground. At tree-top level, the controllers themselves would have no contact with these aircraft, because RT communication equipment functions on the 'line of sight' principle and obstructions block and cut off transmissions.

Radar Tracks (RT) were classified as 'friendly', 'unknown' or 'hostile', based on available flight plans filed for Air Defence Clearances (ADC) issued by the ADDC, the Air Defence Direction Centre. Since no other flying was authorized in the General Area of Hostilities, or GAH, whenever a track came up on the scope for which an ADC number had not been assigned, it was classified as 'unknown' and fighters were scrambled from a nearby base to ascertain the identity of the aircraft and shoot it down if it turned out to be hostile.

Therefore, at any given time, on the radar scope in the Ops Room, affectionately called an 'Igloo', there could be a strike mission going out or returning from across the border, and a PAF air raid striking an IAF base simultaneously.

The base CAP mission if airborne, had to be alerted and vectored onto the incoming enemy aircraft in such cases. IAF fighter aircraft on 'Standby 2' on the ORPs near the runway were also expected to be airborne in two minutes in the event of a 'scramble, scramble, scramble' call on the Tannoy and guided to engage the incoming enemy fighters in combat.

Simultaneously, Air Defence Anti-Aircraft Guns had to be alerted and 'freed' so that they could open up and take on the enemy aircraft, and in addition to all this, PAF RT conversations had to be monitored continuously.

Reports of 'sightings' and 'aircraft sound heard' coming in from the railway station network had to be plotted on maps and correlated with possible targets, and the civil defence organization alerted accordingly about impending air raids, so that civilian movement and vehicular traffic could be brought to a standstill in the target cities and towns.

All these activities had to happen simultaneously, within a matter of minutes, while the rise and fall of the shrill air raid siren repeated many times over, sent a thrill down multiple spines, and kept everyone on their toes. More so on cold winter nights, when the mandatory dusk-to-dawn blackout was routinely enforced across the whole of Punjab.

There were also the tense 'fighter sweeps' flown by our own aircraft over enemy territory, once air superiority was established. These were aimed at drawing out and engaging

PAF fighters in dogfights, which could then be bounced or attacked by escorting fighters waiting above. These would be tense, unpredictable affairs, because no one knew exactly how, or in what numbers, the PAF would respond.

Or if they would respond at all!

The anti-aircraft guns located in a protective ring around the airbase were controlled by the respective sector commanders of the army and apart from relying on the information received from the air force, they also had their own observation posts or OPs. These guns were either 'tight' or 'free' to fire, depending on whether friendly or hostile aircraft were overflying their area of responsibility. When the guns were 'free', they had the authority to target and shoot down aircraft on which they had no prior information, and which had been visually identified as hostile. The barrage of gunfire was huge, especially at night, when myriad gun flashes lit up the dark night sky, in a late Diwali.

Adding to the overall difficulty level in identification of aircraft was the fact that it was freezing cold in north India at the time and a thick fog enveloped the operational area, drastically reducing visibility, and making identification extremely difficult.

This increased the 'clutter' on the radar scopes and interfered with 'pick up' on approaching aircraft. It also created a strange, confusing phenomenon where radars started picking up the tracks of heavy artillery shells flying to and fro across the border, creating uncertainty on whether these were shells, or low-flying aircraft.

Much of this was happening for the first time in an actual war scenario and sometimes led to mix-ups and frayed tempers. It often called for quick and innovative thinking and anticipation from the controllers, since no detailed briefings or precedents were possible or available on many of these situations. This was particularly so with regard to identification of friendly and enemy aircraft and for the 'fighter sweeps'. On these, the controllers dared not keep their aircraft flying on the same course or at the same altitude, for more than a couple of minutes at a time, to guard against sudden pop-up attacks by enemy aircraft, missiles or anti-aircraft guns.

On one such sweep, the MiG-21 pilot, Wing Commander A.K. Singh, flying over the town of Gujranwala at an altitude of 6 km, poignantly asked Control for permission to 'get down low', so that he could take a closer look at his erstwhile hometown before Partition. Since the PAF seemed uninterested in getting into a scrap, permission was duly given by the Radar Controller, and he made two low-level passes over the land of his forefathers.

Bounty says, 'for the first three days of the war, I was on duty twenty-four hours a day and didn't sleep at all, except for dozing off for a few minutes in a chair in the underground Radar Ops Room. Thereafter, another experienced Controller, Flight Lieutenant (later Air Marshal) 'Bill' Mahadik, joined us and we shared overall responsibility of the radar shifts and could each manage to catch a few hours of sleep on a camp cot placed at the back of the Ops Room. Calls from my wife and other families were answered by junior crew members on the shift, to say that we were all doing fine. And this continued for two weeks, till the war ended. It was a crazy, impossibly busy, perpetually on-our-toes time!'

'We hardly had time to breathe, where was the time to be afraid?' he adds.

But this is what they had been trained for and they enjoyed it hugely. For most of them, war was a thrill, a tremendous adrenaline rush. And it was the same with the pilots, who simply got into their aircraft and took off on operational missions, doing what was necessary to keep the aircraft flying, just as they would in routine training sorties. There was a job to be done and the workload was so complex that it did not allow any time for stray thoughts.

After the first three days, or so, they had got somewhat used to the unnerving rise and fall of air raid sirens even in the dead of night, and to the sound of falling bombs, and could tell the difference between exploding bombs and anti-aircraft gunfire. On the fourth morning, in an ill-advised show of youthful bravado, a few of them decided to come out of the Ops Room to look at a PAF Starfighter attacking the base in a daylight raid. Within no time, bullets were raking up the earth around them, as they dived for cover to the ground. Fortunately, no one was hit, and as the Starfighter completed its overhead pass and started to turn around and align itself all over again, it gave them time to scramble back to the safety of the Ops Room, egos bruised, rueing the mindless swagger that had nearly cost them their lives.

Importantly, they all lived to tell the tale!

The next day was by far the most eventful day of the war for them at the Radar unit. Early in the morning, there was yet another incoming raid, with the Pak F-104 Starfighter swooping low over them, trying yet again, to hit the radar aerial and put it out of action. But on this day, his luck finally ran out and the aircraft was shot down by the anti-aircraft guns deployed around the base. The Pakistani pilot ejected from his stricken aircraft and was taken POW. He was saved in the nick of time from the ire of the villagers by personnel from the radar unit and safely brought back to the base for preliminary interrogation.

Amazingly, the pilot turned out to be Squadron Leader Amjad Hussain, (later Air Vice Marshal) who had fought an aerial battle with Squadron Leader A.B. Devaiah, MVC (Posthumous), flying a Mystere over Sargodha in the 1965 war. Amjad had ejected safely from his Starfighter on that occasion too, after being hit by Devaiah's guns, although his aircraft was written off.

Later, he would tell his captors that their radar had always been a thorn in the flesh for the PAF, and he had personally made three unsuccessful attempts on different days, to knock it over, including that first raid on 3 December, which started the hostilities. Frustrated to find it still operating despite repeated attempts, he decided to fly at a lower altitude and a slower speed on this day (the Starfighter was capable of speeds of Mach 2, or twice the speed of sound), in order to give himself a better chance of hitting it, but in the process became an easy target for the anti-aircraft gunners who brought him down.

The same evening, when the captured Pakistani pilot was being airlifted to Delhi for further interrogation in an IAF Dakota, the Amritsar airfield came under attack by PAF B-52 bombers, and runway lights had to be switched off. Despite being asked to return to dispersal and switch off, the daring Dakota pilot decided to continue with his take-off in complete darkness, amidst falling bombs and flashes of ack-ack guns going off around the airfield, leaving the panic-stricken Pakistani pilot screaming at him, 'You're mad! You'll get us all killed.'

For a moment no one on the ground knew where the Dakota was, till he finally called up on R/T after some time, to report calmly that he was 'safely airborne and setting course for destination'.

And all the while, he had kept a pistol pointed at the prisoner, warning him to sit still and not try anything funny!

This was the kind of rough and ready mindset that prevailed at the time, and people really did not think much about personal safety, just getting on with the job at hand.

Late that evening, radar controllers monitoring PAF aircraft radio, picked up transmissions of a fighter being guided with precise instructions by PAF radar, onto what could only be an IAF transport aircraft that had gone over on an unknown mission.

They could hear the PAF pilot confidently saying that he was lining up for his shot and was seconds away from releasing his missiles.

Bounty picks up the story, 'I was in-charge of the radar shift at the time and since the situation appeared desperate for the IAF aircraft, I asked my controllers to start giving repeated blind calls on all available frequencies, asking the "IAF aircraft over Pasrur Ridge to duck down to treetop level", which essentially meant getting down as low as he dared, to evade the PAF Mirage-3 fighter, which was about to shoot him down.

There was no response, but we continued giving those blind calls and after a while we could hear the frustrated PAF pilot angrily telling Control that he appeared to have "lost the b . . ." who had "ducked down".

A little while later we suddenly heard a tentative call from an unknown "mission 206" asking whether it was "safe to climb now". After ascertaining that it was indeed one of ours, an AN-12 transport aircraft on a bombing mission, through the password, counter-password procedures in vogue at the time, we guided him back safely over the border.'

He adds, 'the secrecy around these missions was such that no other radar unit in the vicinity was aware of this mission, and no one knew who the pilot was, or what target he had been tasked to hit. Neither had the aircraft given us a call, as strike missions usually did after getting airborne, so we were just not aware of its existence at all.'

'But I am so glad that we picked them up that day,' he continues, 'thanks to our alertness in monitoring PAF RT, and it was a huge relief when he finally gave us that call, asking for permission to climb.'

The curiosity remained however, and more than forty years later, he came to know by chance, that the call sign 'Mission 206' belonged to one of the Flight Commanders of No. 44 Squadron flying AN 12s, and after a painstaking search, he was finally able to locate and get in touch with him through an email provided by the Delhi Gymkhana Club, where the pilot was a member.

By then however, Group Captain Gursaran Singh Ahluwalia, who was awarded a Vir Chakra for his daring low-level bombing raids, was living in the US, but he still recalled vividly, and acknowledged gratefully, the alertness, that saved his aircraft and lives of the crew that fateful night.

The two have remained in touch ever since.

Air raids declined sharply after 9 December with PAF generally restricting itself to carrying out defensive surveillance around their own airfields, and in support of their beleaguered army. Their serviceability rates had dropped drastically, since a lot of their technicians were Bengali Muslims from erstwhile East Pakistan, some of whom had defected. There were huge trust issues within the PAF and it was felt that given the very real possibility of East Pakistan becoming an independent nation, the loyalty of these technicians and even some of the pilots, towards Pakistan, was questionable.

And this severely curtailed the operational capability of the PAF to strike and bomb Indian targets, after just three or four days of war.

On the other hand, the IAF enjoyed extremely good serviceability rates for their aircraft and other equipment, giving them crucial technical superiority throughout the war.

Compounding this was the fact that the IAF had achieved complete Air Superiority in the Eastern sector within the first days of the war and had bombed PAF airfields and runways and hit aircraft on the ground, putting them out of action.

Intelligence inputs available to Indian forces at the time, suggested that there was only one squadron of F-86 Sabres operating from East Pakistan, based at the airbase at Tejgaon near Dhaka. The IAF, on the other hand, had deployed as many as ten squadrons in the east. However, the Pakistani aircraft had other airbases at Chittagong, Comilla, Jessore, Cox's Bazar etc., to fall back upon, and operate from, when their original mother base was bombed.

But in spite of all this and the pre-emptive strikes carried out by PAF on Air Force Station, Kalaikunda near Calcutta, in the first days of the war, the IAF achieved a complete and resounding victory in the air in no time.

Once that happened, it was the beginning of the end of the air war in the East, and the 10 IAF Squadrons with their associated manpower and equipment, quickly shifted to the western border, dealing a body blow to an already crippled PAF.

The writing was well and truly on the wall by then, as the IAF flew daring missions deep into enemy territory, delivering one devastating strike after another. And in addition to the daytime attacks by Su-7 fighter-bombers and Canberras, even AN-12s switched from a transport to a bombing role. In addition to the Mig-21s, the ageing Mysteres and Vampires and the Hunters and Gnats of the 1965 war, were all pressed into service, to hit so-called 'Targets of Opportunity' deep inside Pakistan. The IAF went over relentlessly in waves, by day and night, and literally threw everything, including the proverbial kitchen sink at them.

By night, AN-12s flew bombing missions, while single aircraft from TACDE, the Tactics and Combat Development Establishment, strafed airfields continuously, denying them opportunity to work on repair of damaged runways under the cover of darkness.

The PAF knew it was beaten.

After the Instrument of Surrender was signed on 16 December in the Eastern Sector, the next morning, IAF SU-7s based at Adampur, carried out one final attack on the Lahore railway yard, leaving their calling cards, so to speak, on the last day of the war, before West Pakistan finally surrendered. They caused extensive damage and stamped complete authority and dominance over a thoroughly demoralized force, in a final, devastating coup de grâce.

The air warriors finally went back home to their families after hostilities had officially ceased on the Western Front on 17 December. In most cases, these men had left home on the afternoon of 3 December, and not returned since.

But the civilian population had looked after the families well in the interim and ensured that the military wives and children were not left alone to fend for themselves, while their menfolk were away fighting for the country . . . In endearing gestures that reflected the spirit of nationalism prevalent at the time, civilian families either invited them over to stay in their homes, or sent women and children from their families, to stay with the military wives and children, at night. People regularly brought over food and other essentials from their homes for them, and for soldiers travelling in trains at railway stations, considering it an honour to be able to do their bit for the men in uniform.

The whole country had come together in a way that would be difficult to imagine in today's times. But war does that to people, stirring up a nationalistic fervour unimaginable in peace time.

It unites and brings people together as nothing else ever can.

And that symbolized the 'Spirit of 1971', as we swept to a euphoric victory and a new country was born.

7

The Forming of the Thunderbolts (1981–82)

'The 9-aircraft formation rolls slowly to the right and pulls sharply downward in a full loop, the aircrafts seemingly glued to each other and pulled by an invisible chord, as the admiring audience on the ground gasps and breaks into spontaneous applause. Like Birds of Prey, they perform numerous sharp turns, dives and climbs, and their vertical loops and rolls especially leave the audience enthralled, as they streak across the sky, billowing thick white smoke trails in their wake, just 8 feet separating the wing tips.'

This is how a 1982 brochure describes a display by the Thunderbolts, the Indian Air Force's first Formation Aerobatics Display Team, in an apt recounting of the mesmerizing display of precision flying that brought the crowd to its feet every time.

This is the fascinating story of how the Thunderbolts was formed.

When Air Chief Marshal Dilbagh Singh, the first IAF pilot to be chosen to convert to the supersonic MiG-21s in late 1962, took over as Chief of Air Staff in 1981, he felt that the most compelling way in which the IAF could showcase itself and win over the hearts and minds of people in its Golden Jubilee year in 1982, would be a breathtaking display of synchronized, high-speed aerobatics performed by a group of colour coordinated aircraft flying in close formation. From the ground, these aircraft would appear as if joined to each other by an invisible thread, literally riding on each other's wingtips.

And so the idea of an IAF Formation Aerobatics Display Team was born, similar to the famous Red Arrows of the British Royal Air Force, to mark the Golden Jubilee Celebrations of the IAF.

In the fifty years since 1932, the IAF had never had an official Formation Aerobatics Display Team, although No. 7 Squadron, The Battle Axes, an elite Hunter squadron, that had distinguished itself in the 1965 and 1971 wars, had formed its own nine-aircraft Formation Aerobatics team way back in 1964–65, under its then Commanding Officer, Wing Commander (later Air Chief Marshal) L.M. 'Baba' Katre.

But it was an individual squadron effort and did not represent the IAF as a whole.

This was to finally change in mid-1981 when the IAF's first Formation Aerobatics Display Team was created under the leadership of Wing Commander (later Air Marshal) P.S. 'Ben' Brar, as the first Commanding Officer.

Time was extremely short and identifying a suitable aircraft for the Display Team was of paramount importance. The ageing British Hawker Hunter that had been the backbone of the IAF fighter fleet in the 60s and 70s, was about to complete nearly twenty-five years of service in the IAF, but still seemed the obvious choice for this historic endeavour. Classically streamlined, it was a beautiful aircraft blessed with superb handling qualities and had been the IAF's premier ground attack fighter over the years.

Given its 1950s vintage however, maintenance and serviceability were always going to be a challenge. And there could be absolutely no compromise or margin of error on 100 per cent serviceability, in an occupation as hazardous as Formation Aerobatics.

It was equally important to have a dynamic and capable team leader who would not only take up the task of forming the team from scratch, but also develop and execute the routines to be flown, in a way that would showcase all that was best about the IAF.

After due deliberations, Air HQs finally decided on Wing Commander P.S. Brar, popularly known as 'Ben Brar', as the best man for this role. He was then commanding No. 29 Squadron at Air Force Station, Jamnagar, and as a young Flying Officer, had been a part of that fabled No. 7 Squadron nine-aircraft Formation Aerobatics team of the 60s, that was a precursor to this dream.

As had been my cousin, Flight Lieutenant Tapan Kumar Chaudhuri.

No. 20 Squadron, known as the 'Lightnings', was chosen for this prestigious assignment and fittingly, the Display Team was named 'The Thunderbolts'. Initially formed in mid-1981, the Thunderbolts were officially in existence as the IAF's elite Formation Aerobatics Display Team from 1982 to 1990.

It was an ambitious venture, undertaken at very short notice with an ageing aircraft that was almost on the verge of being phased out of the IAF. But there was quiet confidence as the squadron moved to Air Force Station, Hashimara, popularly called 'Hashi' in IAF circles, from Air Force Station Hindon near Delhi.

The Thunderbolts would be the last hurrah for the Hunters, after a glittering run in the IAF.

No. 27 Squadron, also flying Hunters, moved to Hashimara from Jamnagar at the same time, to supplement and support the efforts of the Lightnings. In the normal course, the creation of such an elite team would take close to two years in most cases. But the Thunderbolts had less than half that time before the show was to take to the skies for the golden jubilee.

It was a huge challenge and to succeed, everyone involved needed to be at the top of their game.

Fifteen pilots were initially attached to the squadron and each of them flew with the Commanding Officer, in two-aircraft screening sorties, with the first sortie taking off from Hashimara on 30 June 1981. And by August, much of the final team was in place. The selected pilots initially commenced flying three and four-aircraft practice formations, without the aerobatics.

It was obvious from the beginning that not everyone would have the temperament and skill to fly such tight, close formations that called for extreme precision and courage, and complete, unwavering focus at all times. Even the smallest deviation from standard procedures and pre-decided positions and routines could prove to be critical and jeopardize the safety of the entire team.

Not to mention people on the ground.

In the Commanding Officer's own words, 'Formation Aerobatics requires perfect coordination, sharp, split-second reflexes and decision-making and above all, hours of practice that allow the pilot to do the right thing without conscious thought.'

That pretty much summed up the stringent requirements for this hugely demanding task.

Initial selection was for the four primary members of the formation, with Wing Commander Ben Brar out in front and Flight Lieutenant Keshav G. Bewoor (later Air Vice Marshal and inevitably, known as 'KGB') and Flight Lieutenant Kulmeet Singh, fondly called 'Kilo', on his left and right side, respectively, on the Echelons, as wingmen. Deputy Leader Squadron Leader (later Group Captain) J.S. 'Munna' Thakur was just behind him in the Line Astern No. 2 position. These four aircraft formed the basic diamond shape of the formation. The initial practices with these four members went well and soon it was time to add two more, graduating to a six-aircraft display that could execute most of the planned flying routines efficiently.

At this stage, Wing Commander Brar was sent to the UK to do a short stint with the RAF Red Arrows Display Team for orientation and experience. The British team leader was astonished when he learnt that the IAF was raising a display team on Hunters, which the RAF had phased out in the early 1970s and planned to fly a nine-aircraft formation within a time frame of just five months (effectively from September 1981 to mid-January 1982).

He thought it was an impossibility, and did not shy away from saying so in as many words

History, however, bears witness to the fact that he reckoned without the skill and determination of the IAF, and of the Thunderbolts, in particular.

The Commanding Officer's return from the UK in September 1981, sparked off hectic activity in the Thunderbolts' hangers and crew rooms, as aircraft were readied, and diagrams of various formations and routines were drawn and discussed animatedly. The pilots commenced practising formation aerobatics in smaller formations of two to three aircraft initially, and soon graduated to flying six-aircraft routines by November.

Videos were constantly shot from the ground, to see how the formation looked in the air, and identify any shaking, wobbly tails and gaps that needed to be corrected, as the routines were put together and built up. The footage was thoroughly analysed and discussed threadbare at detailed debriefs, especially when there was no flying because of bad weather, which was often in Hashimara.

Whenever the weather was fine, the CO went round in his Jonga, picking up his men to go flying. Progress was rapid, and amazingly, the Thunderbolts took to the skies in their first nine-aircraft formation on Boxing Day in December 1981, a period of less than six months from inception. It was truly a landmark day in their journey.

But it was only the beginning.

Things moved quickly thereafter, and the first official nine-aircraft display was showcased in February 1982 at Air Force Station, Hindon, less than eight months after Wing Commander Brar flew his first sortie at Hashi. This was a spectacular achievement by any standards, which most air forces would not even have attempted, as borne out eloquently by the Red Arrows team leader's scepticism.

A typical display would comprise six aircraft getting airborne in two batches with a time lag of six seconds and then performing twenty different manoeuvres in a dizzying span of eighteen minutes. The formations climbed, dived, turned, criss-crossed each other's flight paths, disappeared into the skies in steep, dizzying climbs, got onto their backs at the top of the climb and accelerated downward in a screaming, edge-of-the-seat dive that left spectators gasping for breath.

The formations or routines that the Thunderbolts flew in the initial years, were named, Shockwaves, Diamond, Inverted Wine Glass, Yankee, etc., each representative of the shape being etched by the formation in the sky. The show culminated in the spectacular Bomb Burst, where the aircraft would enter a screaming vertical dive in formation, and level out and scatter in all directions at the last minute, just as they seemed certain to fly into the ground.

Maintenance Issues

For successful formation aerobatics flying and the achievement of desired levels of precision, it was of paramount importance that the team members and particularly the team leader, should fly the same aircraft each and every time. This was a tall order for this fleet of ageing aircrafts that had almost reached the end of their service lives, but one that simply had to be met.

In the initial days, the junior-most of the Squadron's engineering officers, Flying Officer (later Group Captain) Gautam Dasgupta, who directly worked on the aircraft in the Daily Servicing Section or DSS, recalls that it was a challenge to put up even five or six serviceable aircraft on the tarmac. Getting nine or twelve aircraft ready for a demanding formation aerobatics display was obviously a far cry at that stage. Many of the unserviceable aircraft had not flown for a long time and for the first few days, only two or three aircraft would start up, and the rest would just not respond. The problem was compounded by the high humidity at Hashimara, which very adversely affected the underpowered internal battery of the Hunters. This became a very major difficulty for the Thunderbolts.

But the tenacity and never-say-die spirit of the technical officers and aircraft technicians won the day. Flying Officer Dasgupta, or 'Dasu' as he was fondly called, circumvented the problem by devising external battery carts, much like the ones used for the heavy bombers of World War II, the Lancaster and Liberator especially, and these worked beautifully. Soon they had an adequate number of aircraft proudly lined up on the tarmac for training sorties, and subsequently for the nine-aircraft shows, on a regular basis.

The Commanding Officer himself flew forty-two sorties in December 1981 alone, in his favourite aircraft, bearing tail No. BA 467. Usually, a fighter pilot would not do more than twenty to twenty-five sorties in a month.

From the baby steps of those uncertain early days, the 'Mission Impossible' of 100 per cent serviceability for an entire year of non-stop practices and displays in the Golden Jubilee Year, was achieved without a single incident. It was a miracle and eloquent proof of the unstinting commitment and innovativeness of the technical team who just refused to look at impossibilities.

And for that superlative effort Flight Officer Dasgupta was honoured with a Vishisht Seva Medal, a Presidential Award very rarely given to someone so young, both in terms of age and length of service. An award that he had rightfully earned and richly deserved for his unswerving commitment and determination that kept the aircraft flying, day after day.

In a way it was also the story of the Thunderbolts and what they achieved against all odds, in that incredibly short period of time.

The time of the year chosen for the creation of this elite unit did not make things any easier, since the entire build up to the actual displays happened during the heavy monsoon of 1981. Nestling in the lap of the mighty Himalayas, surrounded by miles and miles of picturesque, lush green tea gardens, Hashimara was right at the heart of the tea country of Dooars in West Bengal, next to the iconic Jaldapara National Park, famous for its one-horned rhinoceros. It was also known for its near-continuous rainfall that went on and on till almost the end of October.

This heavy rainfall meant that the Thunderbolts had to seize every clear day, or part of a day, to fly and work on their training regimen and build up the various routines and formations. But there were plenty of frustrating times, when it was pouring outside and they just could not get off the ground, spent sipping cups of tea in the Crew Room instead.

In hindsight however, Hashimara proved to be a great location for the Thunderbolts, since other than the flying, the sheer isolation of the base meant that there were hardly any other distractions, barring the odd trip, to Siliguri town or Dhulabari on the Nepal border, famous for its market of 'foreign' goods.

This helped to bring the young team members and their families close because they were always together, in and out of each other's houses as a group, in potlucks and coffee-mornings, birthdays and anniversaries, and the Dining Outs and Station Parties that make for such a rich and vibrant social life, even at the most isolated of Air Force Stations. Since military flying is inherently a stressful activity and most bases are secluded and away from civil society, the families of the officers and men are always actively associated and involved in the social fabric of the base.

Families come together to support each other not just in good times, but even more so during the tense, testing times of personal anguish, when a unit moves to a battle zone and an aircraft is reported missing, or worse, when a talking, laughing young man or woman comes home in a coffin draped in the tricolour, with his/her peak cap on top.

For the Thunderbolts, it made for the great bonding and team spirit that is imperative for the success of such high-performance teams, especially since their very lives depended on each other, literally. The easy camaraderie, respect and trust that they shared, bore the signature and stamp of a highly successful, close-knit team, which is essential, since it is just not possible to function in such stressful environments without it.

And it also made for a great atmosphere, especially for the youngsters, that was intensely professional, and yet informal at the same time.

The pilots came from different squadrons and units, from all over the IAF, from different types of aircraft, most of them far more technically advanced than the ageing Hunters that they were now flying in the Thunderbolts. They came from the latest generations of MiGs and Mirages, Jaguars and even Kirans, used for training flight cadets at the Air Force Academy. But once they landed up at Hashimara, the differences in their flying backgrounds became redundant, as they participated day in, day out, in an intense group activity requiring tremendous skill, precision, confidence, and total commitment.

And of course, complete interdependence on each other.

It was vital therefore, that they should be like family to each other, to help withstand that intensity and pressure. Tenures were kept fairly short for the same reason, two or two-and-half years at the most, and there was a constant churning and turnover, of new pilots being inducted and trained as per a laid down syllabus that readied them for flying in specific positions in the close formation displays. The older pilots who had finished their tenures would leave with memories for a lifetime, of a difficult job, well done.

Air Vice Marshal Shyam, then a young Squadron Leader, and one of the key members of the initial Thunderbolts team, flying in the crucial Line Astern 3 slot, immediately behind the Leader and Deputy Leader, remembers practice formations being flown every day on good weather days. Often, the families would be watching from the rooftops of their homes in the Station Married

Quarters. Having watched the formations many times, they knew well the slot in which their husband/dad was flying and were so familiar with the routines that they could actually tell when their loved one was not performing at his best.

And many a time, after the regular squadron debrief, there would be another accurate debrief after a morning of flying, delivered by the ladies at home, along with lunch!

And this complete involvement and participation from everyone was one of the inherent strengths of the Thunderbolts, that helped make them so successful within such a short time, even with a previous generation aircraft that most modern air forces had already phased out.

When the team was getting ready for its first nine-aircraft display at Hindon, one of its earliest audiences included an enthusiastic Prime Minister, Indira Gandhi, accompanied by the Chief of the Air Staff, Air Chief Marshal Dilbagh Singh. Enthralled by their performance, permission was readily given to showcase the Thunderbolts to the country, in a six-aircraft formation over Rajpath and Rashtrapati Bhawan on Republic Day 1982, followed by a nine-aircraft display over Tilpat Range.

The Thunderbolts, flying from Air Force Station, Palam, were scheduled to perform a spectacular vertical Double Loop and Bomb-Burst over Rajpath that day.

But it was not to be, unfortunately.

The week around 26 January is usually the coldest in Delhi, notorious for its dense fog and poor visibility. As it turned out, it was impossible for anyone to fly that morning and the much-awaited Republic Day flypast had to be called off due to bad weather.

Rajpath was not visible from the air!

However, the Chief Guest, the King of Spain, graciously took time out and met the Thunderbolts on 28 January.

This was the first of many scheduled Displays that were to be flown that year as a team of twelve hunter aircraft painted in the distinctive dark-blue-and-white livery of the Thunderbolts went around the country in a succession of spectacular performances at almost every major IAF base. It was an amazing achievement, even more so when seen from a technical standpoint.

The Jaam Sahab of Nawanagar had personally invited them for an air show at Jamnagar and came down from London to watch the spectacular display. The crew were put up in the palace and treated like royalty. They performed overseas in Sri Lanka but a show in Bangladesh was cancelled at the very last minute because of political reasons. They spent almost the whole of that year on the road, flying two to three back-to-back displays every week, across the length and breadth of the land.

As their reputation spread, requests for displays in other countries began to pour in and their first overseas performance at Colombo, Sri Lanka, spread over two days was done for the first time over the open sea at Galle Face. It was a huge success.

Suddenly they were stars.

Everyone wanted to see them, meet them, and shake their hand.

The hitherto unseen 'ballet in the skies' brought tears of joy and pride to the eyes of grown men.

For the Thunderbolts, it meant living out of suitcases for months on end, away from the families, who would sometimes fly down to the most important shows. Air Vice Marshal Shyam, still fondly remembers seeing his infant daughter for the first time, a full month after she was born at the Air Force Hospital in Hashimara. The first news that he had of her was the Hospital CO calling him up to inform him of the birth, just prior to his getting airborne for yet another show.

He remembers the continuous effort, as if it were yesterday. 'Fly to a place, do a practice or two to familiarize with the local features, often doubling up as a dress rehearsal for the station personnel and their families, and school children. Fly in the main display the next day with the entire town turning up to watch, meet local dignitaries, debrief, and fly off to the next stop.'

It meant ferrying an ageing fighter carrying almost no Navaids through cloud and haze, to another part of the country, thousands of kilometres away. Two or three aircraft flying together in loose formation, fervently hoping they had read their navigation charts right, and that the radio compass would lock on to their waypoints, giving them the right headings to fly that would get them there.

This part was sometimes more stressful than the actual display itself, which had been practiced over and over again.

There would usually be a very small gap between two shows and the formation had very little leeway to absorb any delays, due to bad weather, or other reasons. They simply had to be at the destination, in time for the next display.

Flying Officer Dasgupta and his team of thirty-odd technicians, also travelled to every destination in a separate aircraft, usually an AN-12 or a Fairchild Packet or Avro, and did a grand job in keeping the Thunderbolts flying, day after day. 'Dasu' in particular, stood out and had to be literally shooed away from the aircraft and sent home on occasions!

As the number of displays in the Golden Jubilee celebrations of 1982 increased, Wing Commander Brar realized that it would be logistically impossible to move around the length and breadth of the country with a huge back-end contingent of nearly seventy-five technicians who each worked on a separate aircraft system or equipment. So this time-honoured, maintenance standard operating procedure was modified and replaced by one of multitasking by a much smaller handpicked group of thirty-odd technicians, each carrying out multiple functions on the aircraft, led by Dasu.

Again, this was something that had never been tried before.

Today, long retired, Group Captain Dasgupta fondly recalls how, besides carrying out routine first-line maintenance, the technical team often took up night-long repairs and 'second line' servicing as well, to cope with the non-negotiable task of keeping the aircraft flying for the next practice and the next show. There were occasions, when an engine change had to be taken up overnight, to enable an aircraft to ferry out to another base the next morning.

So, they simply worked through the night, till it was done!

He also remembers the challenge of generating the perfect, even, smoke trails that each aircraft needed to emit during the displays. It initially took a gang of four technicians, two hours, to get an aircraft ready and 'smoking' well. But every aircraft had varying smoke emission rates, which needed to be standardized for the smoke trails of the entire formation to look the same. It was a problem that needed a lot of thought and innovation, but like everything else with the Thunderbolts, even this was achieved with élan, and they soon got so used to the process that after each display, a single technician could refill the smoke fluid tank in an aircraft in a matter of ten minutes.

The final team of pilots that went around the country that year, flying nine-aircraft formations with their Team Leader Wing Commander Brar, included Squadron Leader J.S. 'Munna' Thakur as Deputy Leader, and Squadron Leader Shyam flying Line Astern two and three, behind him. Flight Lieutenant Kulmeet Singh and Flight Lieutenant K.G. Bewoor were on the right and left Echelons, diagonally behind the leader as his wingmen, and Flight Lieutenants Randhawa, S.S. Sawhney, P. Kumar and V.P. Singh behind them in the 'outer' positions.

The standby pilots were Squadron Leader G.R. Mallesh and Flight Lieutenants A.R. Nigam, A. Gupta and V.K. Bali.

A key member of that initial Thunderbolts team, Flight Lieutenant (later Group Captain) Kulmeet Singh or 'Kilo' as he was called, who had been with the Thunderbolts right from inception, still remembers the thrill and satisfaction of flying in this elite formation where your nearest neighbour was a mere 8-ft away from your wingtip. He says your life depended on him holding steady and not wobbling or falling out of position. The satisfaction of that intense teamwork, day after day, is something that will stay with them all their lives, he feels.

He finished his regular term of two years with the Thunderbolts, specializing in flying the right (starboard) Echelon and the No. 2/3 Line Astern positions, before moving on for his Flight Instructors course, and a tenure as a flying instructor at Air Force Academy. He came back subsequently on temporary duty to fly in displays for a while, in his old slot, to help the Thunderbolts tide over a temporary shortage of qualified pilots.

AVM Shyam recollects how, for the first three aircraft, flying one behind the other in Line Astern formation, the aircraft behind would always position itself just below the jet wake of the aircraft in front, with the wake hitting it near the right rudder.

And that whenever they flew at higher altitudes, where a jet engine invariably delivers lesser power because of the lower air density, the pilot would need to adjust his throttle to a higher setting than usual, to achieve the same speeds that he was used to, at lower altitudes. As such, he would always have a lesser reserve of power at his disposal during manoeuvres, which was crucial when he needed to keep up or catch up with the acceleration of the leading aircraft.

He also remembers how the aircraft behind the leader would always need to fly a slightly longer distance in the turns because of their larger radius of turn, while maintaining their relative positions with the leader. This meant flying a little faster than him on the turns, and positioning themselves a little more forward than usual on the vertical loops, especially when the lead aircraft was on its back, sliding into a position just under its belly, so that when the leader accelerated into the dive, they would stay with him and maintain their relative positions perfectly, and not fall back and open up gaps in the formation.

These slight adjustments of the throttle and positioning were all-important for good close-formation flying and had to be absolutely perfect for the formation to fall into place nicely on every manoeuvre. This is where the skill, and precision flying ability, and hours of practice really came in.

The key lay in smooth adjustments, he says, in making very gentle and gradual corrections even when you were out of position. Any sudden, harsh change of position, speed or altitude would make it difficult for the aircraft flying with reference to him, to maintain their relative positions, and unseemly gaps would open up in the formation in no time. These not only looked ugly from the ground but were a potential flight safety hazard as well.

The stability of the formation therefore depended to a large extent on smooth, steady flying by the 'inner core' led by the team leader out in front, and the two-line astern aircraft flying just behind him and the two aircraft on his left and right, on the Echelons. These two aircraft were called the first Starboard (right) Echelon and the first Port (left) Echelon, respectively. Along with the Line Astern aircraft, they needed to hold absolutely steady because the outer aircraft of the formation, would be positioning themselves with reference to them, a mere half a wingspan away.

And because of the domino effect, it would always be harder for the 'outer' aircraft to maintain their positions if the 'inner' core was wobbly, because their own manoeuvring and corrections would then become that much greater, leading to ugly up-and-down oscillations at times, as they struggled to stay in position. All this was practised over and over again, till it looked 'perfect' from the ground.

AVM Shyam adds, 'In formation aerobatics, the aircraft that you are maintaining position with, is for all practical purposes, your master, and you are 'lashed' on to him, so to speak. Holding position relative to him is sacrosanct, which essentially means that till the time he calls out to say that he has a problem or emergency, you continue to fly with him and do exactly as he does. His is the only aircraft that you are concentrating on, and while the remaining aircraft in the formation are in your peripheral vision, they do not actually concern you much in terms of your own positioning.'

This then, was the mantra of smooth formation flying and the Thunderbolts swore by it. So much so, that even when a bird or flock of birds went through the formation while operating at low levels, the lead aircraft made no adjustments or undertook any sudden evasive action. They just kept flying as if nothing had happened.

And all the while, the formation leader would be calling out his commands over the R/T, in a continuous monologue, alerting his formation as he moved smoothly into his next manoeuvre. There would be no acknowledgements from anyone, just the leader passing his commands for everyone else to comply. And if someone had an R/T failure, he would just drop out of the formation, following a pre-decided protocol, because he wouldn't be able to hear the leader's commands anymore and would be flying 'blind', unsure of what the formation was doing next, even though he may have rehearsed it many times before. The show would go on without him.

If it were a nine-aircraft formation, they would continue to fly the whole routine with one aircraft less, leaving his position in the formation, blank, or sometimes two more aircraft would be asked by the Formation Leader to drop out and a six-aircraft formation would be flown, which could execute most of the planned routines equally efficiently.

The onus of taking that call to drop out however, lay on the individual pilot, keeping everyone's safety in mind.

Shyam Sir also recalls that displays flown after noon were always more challenging because of convection currents, which are masses of hot air rising upwards, causing turbulence and interfering with smooth flying. As did low clouds, with their internal convection currents, that invariably peaked around noon, not to mention increased bird activity at low levels. All these made formation flying, post noon, more difficult. The best times were the early mornings and late evenings when the air was smooth with little or no turbulence. He says it was a joy to fly at such times. But keeping in mind the convenience of the audience on the ground, it would often be difficult to schedule air shows at those times.

All good things come to an end and so did that golden year for the Thunderbolts. They carried on with many more dazzling performances over the subsequent years, but the aircraft itself was coming to the end of its service life, after nearly thirty-three years and had to be phased out. The Thunderbolts were finally disbanded in 1990, after eight glorious years in the skies, to make way for a new Display Team, flying a different aircraft.

But the Thunderbolts saga remains an unqualified success story in the history of the IAF. It ushered in a new era of formation aerobatics performed for awestruck audiences. It laid the foundations of a later generation formation aerobatics team named Surya Kirans, who initially flew the Kiran aircraft and moved on to the British Hawks, taking the Thunderbolts legacy forward.

It also inspired a generation of awestruck young people who watched them perform, to join the Air Force with the dream of emulating their heroes.

Today, all of them are long retired, but the thrill and excitement of those spectacular air shows that they were once a part of, still lights up their eyes whenever they talk about those times. And they would give anything, to climb into the cockpit of a sleek, dark blue and white Hunter just one more time, and fly smoothly into their respective slots in the formation, and hear once again the Leader calling out 'roooolling in . . .' on their headphones, as the formation moves seamlessly into its next breathtaking manoeuvre . . .

Showcasing all that was best about the IAF . . .

Even as the audience on the ground gasped and broke into wonderstruck applause.

8

The IAF in the Kargil Operations (1999)

Wing Commander Raghunath Nambiar, in command of the lead Mirage 2000 aircraft equipped with Laser Guided Bombs (LGBs) tasked to hit Tiger Hill, glances impatiently at the crosshairs of the laser designator system in the cockpit, as it slowly settles on the command bunker and seven white tents on the hilltop.

He waits as the Litening Pod of his Mirage 'acquires and designates' and then 'lights up' the hilltop target with a laser beam, while the aircraft is still 15 km away. He dives towards it, levelling out at an altitude of 10 km, or nearly 33,000 feet.

As the aircraft crosses the '8 km inbound' mark, it descends further and the aircraft automatically releases the LGB, the 'smart' bomb that glides smoothly down on the laser beam and wings its way inexorably towards the target. It will take a little over 30 seconds to reach the target, seconds that seem like an eternity to the pilots who have their eyes glued to the small tracking screen in the cockpit.

Time stands still, no one breathes.

And then, the screen erupts in a blinding flash of white light, as the LGB hits with pin-point accuracy. And life goes from 'Tally Ho', signifying target designation to 'Splash' or bomb release, to 'Bull's-Eye' or direct hit, and 'Mission Accomplished' for the pilots, all in the span of a few nerve-jangling minutes.

Later, the images of the laser designator's cross resting on Tiger Hill and the laser guided bomb slamming into the hilltop, would become a first Gulf War like TV moment for the audiences back home, that kept playing on their TV screens on loop as the channels of the so-called 'war correspondents' in the Valley played it ad nauseum.

At the turn of the millennium, this is the new IAF with its state-of-the-art aircraft and 'smart' weaponry, striking with a lethal vengeance from which there can be no escape for the enemy.

The first-ever use of the 'smart bomb' at Tiger Hill, marks the beginning of the end of the air war in Kargil, and the Chief of Air Staff (CAS) is on hand to witness the spectacular moment from the rear seat of a Mirage 2000, filming the mission for damage assessment.

The Mirage formation flies around in the area for a while, waiting for the smoke to clear, and then returns, looking for survivors, but there is nothing left, nothing to be seen.

The camp on Tiger Hill has been wiped out in a show of clinical efficiency by the IAF, marking the high point of the air war, vividly showcasing what 'Operation Safed Sagar' was all about.

The mission planning had commenced two days earlier after a solitary MiG-25 'Foxbat' flew an extensive photo reconnaissance sortie, flying parallel to the LOC on our side, photographing the target, which appeared to be six to seven white tents perched on the hilltop. These images were analysed and detailed inputs given to the Mirages to help them pinpoint the exact locations on their Litening Pod cameras which magnified the target to telescopic proportions.

The preparations were complete.

On the evening of 22 June, the orders came to attack the enemy positions on Tiger Hill the following day.

Take-off is planned at 0630 hours from Air Force Station, Adampur with the strike formation of two Mirages escorted by another two Mirage 2000s from Ambala, providing fighter cover. The two formations rendezvous in the air as planned, and the four aircraft composite formation sets course for the target.

On arrival over the target at Tiger Hill that day however, the pilots find to their consternation that there is a layer of cloud covering the hilltop which precludes the laser beams from reaching the target and 'designating' it to the system, for the laser-guided bombs to operate successfully.

Reluctantly, the pilots turn back and call off the mission.

And the intruders live to fight another day.

The sortie is replanned for the next morning, and this time, the weather is clear.

And the rest is history, a part of IAF folklore.

Smarts and Dumbs

A precision-guided munition or weapon (also known as PGM, 'smart bomb' LGB etc.) is a guided weapon programmed to precisely hit a specific target and minimize the collateral damage that invariably follows with conventional, unguided weapons.

The advent of precision-guided weapons led to the renaming, perhaps a little condescendingly, of older, low-technology bombs as 'unguided bombs', 'dumb bombs', or 'iron bombs'. In the laser-guided technology used for 'smart bombs', the target is first 'lit up' by a laser beam fired from the releasing aircraft, a process known as 'designating' or 'lasing' the target. Sensors in the bomb's nose then lock onto the reflections of the laser beam and the bomb rides or glides on this beam to the target rather than being dropped on it, giving it the precision capability to hit tiny, pinpoints such as individual bunkers or tents, or a bridge, with unerring accuracy.

Targets that would have otherwise required the use of hundreds of tonnes of ordnance—the normal 'unguided' or 'dumb' bombs—in the old-fashioned carpet or area bombing tactics of World War II for successful destruction . . .

With the associated collateral damage.

The other benefit is that the aircraft launching the LGBs are also at less risk from anti-aircraft guns. Smart bombs can be released while still some distance away from the target as standoff weapons, as opposed to the vulnerable, low-level, dive-bombing runs over the target through heavy anti-aircraft gunfire, that were necessary in the past.

LGBs were first developed by the United States during the Vietnam War, and quickly proved their worth in precision strikes on difficult pinpoint targets.

Data from an amazing 28,000 laser-guided bombs dropped in Vietnam show that they achieved direct hits nearly 50 per cent of the time, while unguided bombs had an accuracy of just 5.5 per cent per mission.

The USAF and other air forces are now upgrading their LGBs to include an additional GPS guidance as backup. These weapons, in addition to the usual laser designation of targets, now also have a GPS-based inertial navigation system as backup, so that if the laser illumination of the target is somehow lost or broken, the bomb will still continue to home in on the target on the basis of GPS coordinates.

In October 2010, India developed its first LGB, 'Sudershan', at the Instruments Research & Development Establishment (IRDE), a lab of the Defence Research and Development Organisation (DRDO).

LGBs at Kargil

The French Mirage 2000 aircraft acquired by the IAF in the mid-80s, had come equipped with Thomson-CSF laser designator pods known as ATLIS, capable of delivering Matra 1000 kg laser-guided smart bombs, at the time of purchase. However, these bombs were extremely expensive, and were already predesignated for specific targets by the IAF. They would normally not be diverted or used for any other purpose.

Also, the original laser-designator pod (LDP) possessed only daytime capability. Keeping the requirements of a full-scale conflict in mind, this needed to be upgraded to include night capability as well, for which the IAF had already signed a contract with an Israeli company in 1997, two years before Kargil. But this would take nearly three to four years to become operational in the normal course.

Indigenously, the Jaguars were the first IAF aircraft to be modified to carry precision guided weapons in the mid-1990s, when LDPs were integrated with the aircraft.

Therefore, although the basic precision munitions capability and technology was already available to the IAF, well before the Kargil Operations, it needed to be modified significantly to include night capability amongst other things. This was achieved on fast track during the fifty-day war by the IAF, in conjunction with the Israelis, who fitted the Litening Electro-Optical Targeting Pods that provided the LGB system with the desired capability. The Litening pods had a laser 'designator' and a powerful camera, which magnified the view of the target by ten times.

A total of only nine LGBs were used by the IAF during the Kargil War, eight by Mirages, and one by a Jaguar. Of these, four were dropped by Wing Commander (later

Air Marshal) Raghunath Nambiar, a Mirage test pilot temporarily attached to No. 7 Squadron, the 'Battleaxes', for the war, including the very first one that hit Tiger Hill on 24 June 1999.

The bulk of the damage was done however, by dumb bombs, used with great accuracy by the Mirages, thanks to the Litening Pod magnification cameras. The philosophy was to use the smarts only if the dumbs failed to produce the desired results. However, this was seldom the case, and as planned, the IAF used the smarts very sparingly in this war.

All LGBs were delivered by two-seaters or trainer aircraft, with the rear-seat pilot doubling up as a WSO (pronounced 'Vizo'), or a Weapon Safety Officer, and the pilot mainly concentrating on flying the aircraft.

The Litening Pods were fitted with Charged Coupled Device (CCD) and infra-red cameras which were capable of taking highly magnified pictures of the target in real time, and the Mirages were therefore able to locate them easily and produce compelling, pinpoint footage of people running away from the bunkers that they destroyed on Tiger Hill and Muntho Dalo.

The Air War Begins

The Cabinet Committee on Security authorized the IAF to mount attacks on the infiltrators with the rider of not crossing the LOC, on the evening of 25 May 1999, and the Air Force plunged into a full-scale offensive code-named Operation Safed Sagar from the twenty-sixth onwards, with rockets fired from MiG-21s and Mi-17 helicopters in low-level strikes on the first day, hitting Tiger Hill and Tololing. In the light of subsequent events, however, this tactic was to change very quickly.

Flying from air bases at Srinagar and Avantipur, in the Valley, and from Ambala and Adampur, in the plains, ground-attack aircraft, MiG-21s, MiG-23s, MiG-27s, and one MiG-25, one Canberra, Jaguars, and Mirage 2000s swung into action at various times of the conflict, striking enemy positions.

As part of Safed Sagar, there were a total of forty-five IAF aircraft stationed in the Valley at airbases in Srinagar and Avantipur and another forty-five operating from outside the Valley from bases at Ambala and Adampur. The IAF flew a total of 1750 missions over the fifty days of the war, including 1663 daylight sorties. A total of 923 bombs were dropped in the Valley and 234 outside it, in a concentrated effort that brought the enemy to its knees.

In a typical air raid over Kargil by the Mirages, two formations would get airborne simultaneously, the strike or ground attack formation supported by a fighter escort formation providing air defence cover. The Strike would take off from Adampur and the escorts, armed with BVR, beyond visual range missiles, would get airborne from Ambala rendezvous in the air at a pre-designated point, and fly to Kargil where their endurance or fuel limit allowed them to operate for up to one hour and forty-five minutes.

These missions would usually operate at an altitude of 33,000 feet, to stay above the range or 'envelope' of the

Pakistani shoulder-fired Stinger missiles, which were in abundance in the conflict area. Other aircraft based in the Valley would join up with these formations to provide air defence cover when necessary.

The Losses

Even prior to the commencement of Air Operations on 26 May, an IAF Canberra aircraft on a reconnaissance mission on 21 May, had been hit and severely damaged by a Pakistani Stinger missile, although it managed to come back and land safely at Srinagar.

The euphoria of the first day's successful strikes was to be short-lived. The next morning on 27 May, two formations comprising two MiG-27s each, struck a target near Batalik. The first formation was successful, but the leader of the second was unable to press home his attack and had to abort. Both aircraft of this formation then attempted a second attack, again without success. The young No. 2, Flight Lieutenant Nachiketa, then decided to make a third attempt, against laid down norms, and fired his rockets from well above the prescribed height, causing his engine to shut down.

He ejected and landed safely but was taken prisoner and subsequently released after eight days. Nachiketa suffered a serious back injury in the ejection and did not fly a fighter again. He switched to flying transport aircraft and is presently flying for a civil airline after his retirement from the Air Force as Group Captain.

Hearing Nachiketa's ejection call on the radio that day, Squadron Leader Ajay Ahuja, flying a MiG-21 Type 96 fighter on a target-damage, photo-assessment mission, went looking for him, trying to pinpoint the exact landing spot. Probably a little unmindful in the process, he got down too low and put himself within the range of the shoulder-fired Stinger missiles. Sensing their opportunity, the intruders fired a missile at him which locked onto his aircraft and brought him down. Despite a successful ejection, he was surrounded by enemies on the ground, and in a shocking development, tortured and killed. His body was handed over to Indian authorities at a frontier post a few days later.

If this was not bad enough, the next morning a Mi-17 helicopter, part of a four-aircraft formation that had taken off from Air Force Station, Srinagar to attack Point 5140 near Tololing, was also shot down by Stinger missiles. Four gallant air warriors, Squadron Leader Pundir, Flight Lieutenant Muhilan, Flight Sergeant Prasad, and Sergeant Sahu lost their lives in this attack. Unfortunately, their helicopter had not been equipped with the electronic flare dispensers, that would have masked its position, and diverted the missiles locked on to it.

This was tragic, because with their low-operating heights, the slow-moving helicopters were easy targets for the Stingers, and needed to consistently drop flares as a counter measure to save themselves from being hit.

The IAF thus made a disastrous start to the air war, suffering major losses in the first three days. The downing of two fighters and one helicopter on two successive days along with six aircrew, indicated an urgent need for a rethink of tactics, and resulted in a quick raising of the operating heights of aircraft over Kargil. It also led to a withdrawal of the vulnerable armed helicopters to a different role. The newly modified Air Defence Mirages deployed in the war zone in a ground attack role in the first week of June, alongside the Jaguars, would prove to be the turning point.

And an absolute game-changer.

Getting Down to Brass Tacks

The Mirage operations commenced on 7 June with an attack on Point 5140, and while the strike on Tiger Hill by the Mirages made the headlines, the mission that really broke the enemy's back, was the demolition of its major supply dump at Muntho Dalo on 16 June.

Muntho Dalo was the real turning point in the air battle and the Mirages located and hit the well-fortified supply depot, stocking rations, ammunition, and other battle equipment for the intruders occupying the heights in the area. Destroying this post was, therefore, vital for the IAF. The major logistics and supply depot consisting of seventy tents at approximately 14,000 feet, was bombed out of existence, with more than 300 Pakistanis killed in an air attack lasting just six minutes, crippling the source of sustenance of the intruders on the hilltops. The Pakistanis knew that without rations and supplies, the end was near.

This was a huge setback and forced them to retreat into their own country over the next few days.

The high magnification capability of the Litening sensor cameras fitted in the Mirages was utilized to locate this target and dumb 250 kg Spanish bombs from the 1970s were dropped with an accuracy of 20 metres, phenomenal for a dumb. These bombs had originally been procured for the 'Ajeeth' aircraft manufactured by HAL, which had since been phased out of the IAF, leaving the bombs surplus and available for use by the Mirages.

And this pattern of dropping dumbs using the Litening pod cameras to locate targets was the hallmark of almost all subsequent attacks by the Mirages. Since the dumbs could now be dropped with maximum accuracy, the smarts or LGBs were very rarely used. As mentioned earlier, the Mirage 2000, which is originally an air defence fighter meant mainly for air-to-air combat, proved its true worth in this war in a hitherto unused ground attack or bombing role. Its phenomenal accuracy with dumb bombs proved to be such that a Mirage trainer (two-seater) equipped with LGBs, was usually deployed only as backup aircraft at the tail end of a Mirage formation to film the attacks. Its LGB would be used only if the results of the main formation were not up to the mark, which was very rarely the case.

After using LGBs to obliterate the Command and Control Centre at Tiger Hill, the Mirages reverted to the dumbs again in their attacks on Point 4388 in the Drass sector on July 4 and 6, and knocked out enemy supply dumps and gun positions, breaking down the enemy supply chain in that area, shattering their morale.

By 12 July, the war in the air was pretty much over, and there were no more targets left to hit for the IAF.

What had started disastrously for the IAF thus ended in a blaze of glory, thanks mainly to the accurate strike capabilities of the Mirages.

Lessons Learnt and Innovations

Locating a tiny target such as a bunker or a tent from a fast-moving aircraft had hitherto been a huge challenge for the IAF, but the arrival of the Litening sensor with its high-magnification camera, along with other innovations such as GPS, made a big difference to the bombing strikes, especially in poor visibility conditions and at night.

The lessons of the disastrous early reverses were quickly learnt, and all aircraft operated at altitudes between 30,000-33,000 feet), pulling out of their dives and bomb runs well above the range of the Stinger missiles, which fell away uselessly, unable to reach our aircraft.

With this new strategy, hundreds of sorties were flown by the Mirages in support of the Army, with no further casualties or losses after the initial setbacks. This greatly facilitated a gradual takeover of the mountain posts by the Indian troops and there was not a single operation on the ground that was not preceded by an airstrike.

Other than the airstrikes, the IAF, as always, played a massive role in casualty evacuation, and reinforcement of troops, with Mi-17 Helicopters playing a stellar role in this capacity, operating ceaselessly, round the clock. And in a very significant first for the IAF, an Indian woman helicopter pilot flew into a war zone for the first time, breaking a huge gender barrier.

Technical officers and crew, Radar and Air Traffic Controllers and every other air warrior involved in Operation Safed Sagar worked tirelessly, round the clock, to keep the aircraft flying and were in many ways, the real unsung heroes of this operation. The IAF thrives on these unknown air warriors and their complete, unwavering dedication to duty.

The Bombing of Tiger Hill

The bombing of Tiger Hill, however, remains the showpiece of the air war in Kargil. As mentioned earlier, on 24 June, a Mirage 2000 strike mission comprising two aircraft was tasked to hit the command post at Tiger Hill, that was directing fire on Indian troops, with a laser-guided bomb, on 24 June. They were accompanied by a third Mirage 2000, a two-seater, to witness and photograph the event. This mission marked the use of a LGB by the IAF for the first time. Air Chief Marshal A.Y. Tipnis—the then chief of the air staff—had flown into Adampur prior to the sortie and in a daring move, which greatly boosted the morale of the pilots, he occupied the rear seat of the third aircraft and witnessed the attack first-hand.

Wing Commander Raghunath Nambiar or 'Namby', as he was affectionately called, was the pilot in command of the lead aircraft carrying out the attack and the story of the attack on Tiger Hill is best told in his own words:

'I had the target in sight, on my 'scope' well before we reached the weapon release line. We were firing at six-seven white tents on Tiger Hill with one LGB each.

But there was a problem. At 28,000 feet, we had a very strong component of crosswind of almost 70 knots (130 kmph) which could seriously disrupt the accurate delivery of the weapon on to the target.

A quick decision was taken, and we descended to 26,000 feet where the winds were within acceptable limits and flew on towards the target with all systems 'Go' for sending out the bomb to its destination.

I pressed the firing button and the aircraft bucked like a horse—losing 600 kg of weight from its underbelly.

The bombs were on their way and as I turned the aircraft away with my sights slaved to the target, I waited with bated breath looking at the small screen in front of me.

The 30 seconds of the bomb's flight to the target seemed like an eternity and then, Whoosh! The entire screen went white showing the impact on the tents.'

Once the smoke cleared, the Mirages flew over Tiger Hill at a lower altitude to film the area and assess the damage.

Nothing was left on top of the hill. The camp had ceased to exist.

Conclusion

Fast forward to the present. Twinkling Christmas lights light up a peaceful nativity scene as quiet serenity marks a celebration, we take for granted each year at IAF Officers' Messes.

But it is also the moment to think and remember the young bravehearts whose lives were snuffed out forever in the prime of youth, on the frigid, unforgiving heights of Kargil, so that we may have ours.

To think of their young children, now grown, twenty-five years after that war, who lost their dads when their aircraft was shot down in the brutal killing of a senseless war.

And of the loneliness of the unlived years and moments of togetherness that a young family was deprived of.

Those brave young men just happened to be doing their duty to the nation.

To think of the young fighter pilot shot down and surrounded on the ground by a bunch of killers. And of a defenceless, slow-moving helicopter that was a sitting duck for a deadly shoulder-fired missile.

The IAF made a promise to honour and cherish their memories.

A promise that must be honoured in perpetuity.

9

Maldives Ahoy (2004)

Families lazed about in the golden sands of the beach, lounging in deck chairs, while children played in the sand, squealing with joy as a wave climbed higher onto the beach than expected and threw them off their feet.

No one suspected that a monster was at work, lurking beneath the serene aquamarine waters of the ocean.

And then suddenly, out of nowhere, came hell and high water, sweeping away everything before it . . .

Nineteen years ago, on 26 December 2004, Boxing Day, when the world was on holiday in the midst of Christmas and New Year celebrations, a calamitous tsunami swept through the Southern Pacific and Indian Ocean, leaving a trail of death and destruction in its wake, of such massive proportions, as had never been witnessed before.

It washed away entire families and shattered communities, changing thousands of lives forever. In Sri

Lanka, near Galle, an entire trainload of people was swept away in the raging waters.

For an entire generation who weathered the unprecedented devastation and havoc of that day, the sea had turned into a Frankenstein, a monster to be feared.

A seaside holiday conjures up images of a serene blue ocean stretching into the horizon and an endless succession of waves lazily gaining ground on the beach. Of relaxed bare foot walks in the sand, little ripples of water wetting the feet now and then and running away joyfully from the slightly bigger waves amidst squeals of laughter. Of tall drinks and oversized straw hats and rows of deck chairs in the sand.

And large bay windows bringing in the ocean and the sky into luxurious hotel rooms.

But on that fateful day, all of it changed, and nothing would ever be the same again.

For those who saw the monster waves that swallowed up lives, families, homes, and communities, the serenity and fun of a beach, would take a long, long time to come back.

If ever.

This is the story of those dark days, narrated by my batchmate, Group Captain Erat Krishnaprasad, EK to us, who was in the thick of the massive rescue effort that unfolded subsequently.

Batchmates in armed forces parlance are called Course mates and EK was the Best Flight Cadet of our Course. Even today, he continues to be a part of much of the latest advances in Inertial Navigation and Flight Management Systems (FMS) at Honeywell.

This is also the story of an exceptional aircraft, the Avro, the Hawker Siddeley HS 748, which has been in service with the IAF for over six decades. I still remember vividly, our first official air experience as flight cadets at the Air Force Academy, way back in 1986, in an Avro that flew us to Santacruz, and back, from Hyderabad.

We were crowding behind the Captain on the way back, watching the final approach as he brought her in smoothly and landed at AFA, just in time for dinner.

The induction of the Avro into the IAF was largely the result of the dream and untiring efforts of Air Vice Marshal Harjinder Singh, who had initially joined the IAF as a lowly Hawai Sepoy. That story is now a part of the country's aviation folklore, but would bear a mention here. He dreamed the impossible dream of manufacturing an aircraft for the IAF, at Air Force Station, Kanpur, Chakeri, in the late 1950s, as a replacement for the ageing Douglas DC-3 Dakota.

After sifting through various options, he finally decided to go with the HS 748, which was still in the process of being developed at Duxford, UK, under the aegis of the original designers M/s A.V. Roe & Co., which subsequently merged with Hawker Siddeley, which in turn later merged with British Aerospace.

After quickly concluding contractual formalities, in 1959–60, major aircraft assemblies and parts were airlifted from the UK, to a newly-raised IAF unit, called the Aircraft Manufacturing Depot at Chakeri.

The first AVRO 748 assembled in India took to the skies in November 1961, only a few short weeks after the second original prototype had made its maiden flight in the UK, making it only the third AVRO 748 Series 1 aircraft to fly, fitted with Dart 6 engines.

Probably, never again in aviation history, has a user assembled an aircraft that was still in the process of being tested by the designers.

It was named 'Subroto' after the first Indian Chief of the Air Staff, Air Marshal Subroto Mukerjee.

A total of 85 Series 2 aircraft with Dart 7 engines were to be subsequently manufactured at Kanpur, where the Aircraft Manufacturing Depot was merged with HAL in 1964. Seventeen of these were flown by Indian Airlines on commercial short-haul flights, with former Prime Minister Rajiv Gandhi, being one of its prominent pilots.

The IAF, which still has around sixty of these Avros, at the time of writing this story, is finally in the process of phasing them out now in 2023, after sixty years of glorious service, and replacing them with the newly inducted Airbus C-295s.

Which is amazing testimony to the utility and longevity of an exceptional aircraft.

But this is EK's story, and he picks it up from here in a first-person account.

'I was posted as Navigation Leader (or Nav Leader as it was called), of one of the oldest transport squadrons of the Indian Air Force in December 2004—a squadron of Avros, the twin-engine turboprop Hawker Siddeley HS-748 aircraft, known to many as the Queen of the Skies. With the Rhinoceros as part of our Squadron Crest, we, the Rhinos, were a proud and hardy lot.

The HS 748 was the last aircraft to be developed by Avro, before it merged with Hawker Siddeley. And its sleek aerodynamic design enabled it to skim the clouds with an unmatched smoothness that led to its extensive use in flying the Queen of England on short-haul flights in the 1960s.

The aircraft had been inducted into the IAF in 1964. With a cruising speed of 200 knots and a cruising altitude of 15,000 feet, it could carry almost five tonnes of weight. It could fly around 1400 nautical miles or remain airborne for nearly seven hours at a stretch on a single refuelling. It also possessed an exceptional safety record and had flown in every possible terrain, in every conceivable role.

Back then in 2003–04 the aircraft was undergoing a major avionics upgrade and acquiring additional navigational aids that would make it more technology-driven and more efficient to navigate and fly. But on long-haul flights over the sea, the time-honoured method of manually plotting the aircraft's flight path on flight charts, calculating the prevailing winds and fixing the aircraft's exact position at any given time, still remained sacrosanct.

The introduction of Flight Management Systems (FMS) was still some years away for us, although Boeing had already been using them on their B757s and 767s for some time. Today, a Honeywell FMS exists on aircraft as small as the Cessna 182, as part of standard cockpit equipment.

But more about that later.

In most Avro aircraft for civilian use, the navigator's station came with a built-in table and chair. Since ours was an operational squadron with space and weight at a premium, navigators operated from the jump seat near the cockpit door and we actually plotted our courses on a small platform kept over our laps, a precursor literally, to the modern laptops that would come a few years later!

On that fateful Sunday morning, I was busy getting my Navigation Bag in order. Aircraft today have an Electronic Flight Bag (EFB) which stores all essential Nav and flight documents digitally. But twenty years ago, we still carried these as old-fashioned printed paper documents.

Regulations mandated that a navigation bag should contain seventeen items—two sets of 1 million scale maps covering the entire country, approach charts (for guiding aircraft onto the runway for landing), neatly divided into two folders, one for civil and one for military airports, a list of communication frequencies (mostly confidential), a Douglas Mk IV Computer (an old-fashioned instrument with algorithmic rotatable dials that could carry out complex mathematical calculations), a Douglas protractor, a high school geometry box and compass to mark off the distances on the en route charts, a straight-edge scale, and even a regular old schoolboy pencil box.

This onerous activity took up most of the day and occupied my entire attention. In the evening, when I finally went home, oblivious to the fact that the world had turned upside down in the interim, gut-wrenching images of the tsunami were playing on all TV channels. The IAF is usually the first major responder in any natural calamity as personnel, lifesaving equipment, and relief material of all kinds are quickly flown into the affected site. As I looked at those images on TV, I knew this was something that we would be right in the middle of, very soon.

Sure enough, within the next thirty minutes, the phone rang, and my was on the line, detailing what was expected of the Rhinos in the massive rescue effort that had been launched.

The IAF had mustered its entire transport fleet for relief and rescue operations, and a task force had been set up at Air HQs to coordinate and monitor each of those flights. The government had also tasked the IAF to lend a helping hand to our neighbouring countries, including one that is greatly in the news today, the Maldives.

Our biggest transport aircraft, the mighty IL-76 had already landed in Sri Lanka with relief material and other aircraft were soon to follow.

The workhorse AN-32 squadrons had also swung into action. It was now our turn in the Avros, to be on our way.

Our immediate mission was to launch two aircraft to Male, the capital city of Maldives, early next morning. We were to pick up vitally needed relief supplies from Thiruvananthapuram en route and proceed to Male. Both aircraft would return to Thiruvananthapuram and operate from there, for as long as necessary.

A critically important mission of this nature called for meticulous preparation from all concerned, to ensure that everything went well. The engineering officers got busy choosing aircraft that were not due for any immediate servicing. Technicians and ground crew armed with carefully chosen spares were detailed to travel with the aircraft to provide technical backup at off-base locations.

The aircrew worked out the shortest possible routes and planned the minute details of how best to execute their task.

The squadron was a beehive of activity till late that Sunday evening, as the aircraft were readied for a pre-dawn take-off at 0530 hours. Even the civilian ATC at Vadodara, which usually opened at sunrise, would be open at that hour, to facilitate our departure.

By late evening, we were all set and raring to go.

The excitement in the air was palpable as we arrived at the tarmac in the pre-dawn darkness. The CO was himself on hand to coordinate last-minute details and ensure wheels up at 0530 hours.

After obtaining our clearances and the mandatory ATC and meteorological briefings, we walked out to the aircraft for what we all knew would be a long day at work.

The Avro carries a crew of three, a pilot, co-pilot, and a navigator. We finished the external checks of the aircraft and soon climbed into our seats to carry out the rest of the pre-flight checks. In no time we were calling up the ATC for permission to start engines and taxi out for take-off. The clearance came immediately, along with the runway-in-use, prevailing surface winds, and departure instructions. The ATC added a quiet 'Good Luck' at the end of the standard ATC transmission.

Exactly at 0530 hours. we were away and climbing on course to our assigned cruising altitude.

As we winged our way south, it was a long five-hour flight to Thiruvananthapuram and with the aircraft in cruise mode, we suddenly had time on our hands, grateful for the opportunity to open our breakfast packets.

Apart from the general plan of landing at Thiruvananthapuram and picking up relief material, we still had no idea of what to expect from the day ahead.

Upon landing, the relief material consisting of food, water, clothes, blankets, medicines etc., was speedily loaded on to the aircraft. We grabbed a quick bite at the ATC cafeteria and were soon away again at 1300 hours for Male.

Maldives, an archipelago, south of India, is a beautiful holiday destination for people from all over the world. Its serene blue–green waters and calm, natural surroundings, an ocean away from the pressures and bustle of city life, have always been a much-anticipated destination for stressed city folks. It is also a haven for underwater adventure activities like scuba diving and snorkelling. Luxurious hotel rooms jutting right into the open sea in flower-petal configurations looked beautiful from the air.

The capital city, Male, lies 345 nautical miles south of Thiruvananthapuram and is a flight of less than two hours, over the vast expanse of the Indian Ocean. But these same geographical features make it extremely vulnerable in a tsunami. The isolated small islands that make up the tiny country had been almost completely submerged by the high waves, causing death and destruction. The lucky ones survived on a prayer and a desperate hope that they would be rescued and picked up before any subsequent inundations, if and when, they happened.

As for us, we felt safe in our own little bubble in the cockpit, cruising serenely at 15,000 feet, sandwiched between the deep blue skies above and the sparkling waters below.

The line of sight communication of the VHF RT Aircraft radio meant we would lose contact with Thiruvananthapuram airport in about 150 nautical miles at this height, and would have no contact with Male ATC for another fifteen minutes thereafter.

While in this grey zone, we received a call from our No. 2 aircraft saying that the plan had changed mid-air for us, and we were to now land at Hanimadhoo instead of Male.

None of us had heard of Hanimadhoo before and in those manual, pre-FMS/Inertial Navigation days, this sudden change sparked off an animated discussion in the cockpit on whether we should press on to this unknown location in a foreign country without any ground navigation aids, or land at Male and ascertain more details before venturing out into the unknown.

I quickly grabbed my en route charts to see if I could locate this island. These charts, published by Jeppesen Inc., an American company based at Denver, were and still are the lifeline of aviators. But while we swore our lives on Jeppesen, 'Jepps' as they are fondly called, I was not sure that even they would have Hanimadhoo covered!

A few months previously, Jeppesen had given a major facelift to their en route charts and included invaluable additional information such as runway orientation and length, frequencies to contact, watch hours of the ATC etc., against each airport marked on the charts.

If Hanimadhoo was on Jeppesen, we would make it there. Today, Jepps are stored electronically in the EFBs and on the tabs of pilots and can be accessed at the touch of a finger.

Not so then.

So it was a huge sense of relief when I found the tiny island marked in one corner at the very edge of the chart. A small island with just about 4000 feet of runway, less than half the standard runway length of 9000 feet.

Would someone be there in the ATC after the tsunami, we wondered? Was the radio frequency correct? Was it really such a short runway?

We would soon know.

We turned right from our original course and headed towards Hanimadhoo. Over the open sea, in the absence of NAVAIDS on the ground, pilots in those days had to rely completely on the navigator's calculations, and I fervently hoped mine were right.

Now the FMS takes care of all that. The FMS is a specialized computer system that automates a wide variety of in-flight tasks, reducing the workload on the flight crew, to the extent that most modern aircraft no longer carry flight engineers or navigators.

The FMS also accesses the readings of the inflight instruments from the Air Data computer, such as aircraft heading, speed, altitude, etc. It predicts times and speeds required accurately and can determine an aircraft's exact position.

Given the flight plan and the aircraft's position, the FMS calculates the course to fly at every stage of the flight. The pilot can then choose to fly this course manually, or it can be keyed into the autopilot settings and the aircraft literally flies itself to the desired destination.

But all this was some years away for us then, and we still did most of those things manually.

And mistakes could prove to be extremely costly.

As we came closer to the island, we tuned the frequency of Hanimadhoo on the radio and called up the ATC. To our eternal relief, a cheery young voice immediately answered, welcoming us to Hanimadhoo.

We soon sighted the tiny island amid the blue waters and decided to make an orbit over the airport and check out obstructions, prevailing surface winds etc., and then choose the appropriate runway direction for landing. Everything seemed clear, and we were soon on final approach to the tiny runway, touching down smoothly right at the beginning of the runway, at the correct speed, to maximise our braking space before the runway ended.

It sounds simple when I say it like this, but in reality, it takes great skill and precision to execute such landings safely.

Our pilots made it look easy.

The off-loading party was waiting for us. The cargo was quickly transferred onto boats and ferried away to nearby islands in dire need of succour. And we walked over to the tiny ATC to check on our return flight to Thiruvananthapuram.

The ATC officer was Hamid, a young twenty-five-year-old local. His office also doubled up as his home and looked every inch the bachelor's pad that it was, with clothes strewn all over the place and a music system prominently occupying pride of place in the room. I asked, 'Hamid, what was the tsunami like?' He shook his head pensively but said he had received news that all his relatives were safe.

This island and airport had experienced gale-force winds, he said, but luckily there had been no major damage or fatalities. A few of the neighbouring islands of that atoll, however, were badly affected and in need of immediate relief. As he spoke, I realized the dire circumstances that had necessitated the sudden mid-air change of plan for us, and brought us to this tiny island, instead of Male.

The ATC was just one small room equipped with the bare minimum communication equipment and landlines. Usually, an ATC of any size would have at least four to five people in a watch or shift. This airfield had just one. The equally rudimentary fire-fighting services consisting of just one fire tender and one Gypsy, were similarly sparsely staffed.

We chatted with Hamid for a while and then went out and dipped our feet in the now calm waters of the ocean right next to the runway.

The enormity of the sea surrounding this beautiful island, and its sheer isolation and solitude, took our breath away. It was just a tiny, distant dot, lost in the middle of the mighty ocean.

And I wondered at the loneliness of this young man amidst this magnificent natural beauty.

As we walked back to the ATC to bid goodbye to Hamid, there was another surprise waiting for us. This time it was a message from Male ATC, asking us to proceed to Male and not Thiruvananthapuram, as originally planned.

A quick check of the route to be flown and of the fuel on board, and we knew that we could make it to Male comfortably. And so, it was goodbye Hanimadhoo, this tiny island we'd never heard of before, and probably never would again, and on to Male.

By this time, it was already 1600 hours or 4 PM, and our pre-dawn 0530 hours take-off from Vadodara seemed like a lifetime away. There would be just enough daylight for us to refuel at Male and return to Thiruvananthapuram.

Or so we thought.

Our logbooks show that we had already flown eight hours that day. The rules as laid down in the MATO, the Manual of Air Transport Operations, mandate that aircrew are usually allowed to fly six hours in a day and up to a maximum of eight hours.

In exceptional circumstances, this can stretch to ten hours.

These limits have been laid down by experts after much thought, because flying is an extremely tiring and unforgiving business that calls for complete attention and alertness at all times and allows for very little margin of error.

Pilot fatigue dulls reflexes and affects decision-making abilities adversely, which can lead to disastrous consequences and fatalities. Even non-stop trans-continental flights carry additional sets of crew depending on the total flight time, and are replaced on an average, after every five to six hours of flying.

Our second aircraft had already landed in Male by the time we were on final approach and our colleagues received us on the tarmac.

Male is one of the most picturesque airports of the world, surrounded by the sea on all sides. Against the flaming backdrop of the setting sun, I could see several seaplanes parked on the water. A few speedboats were racing away to the nearby island where the administrative capital is located. It looked gorgeous at that moment and seemed to have no connection with the reality of the natural disaster that had brought us here.

The airport was big enough to park eight large passenger planes at a time. As I turned to look towards the departure terminal, I experienced for the first time, the full impact of the effects of the tsunami.

Passengers of different nationalities, who had come here to spend their much-anticipated Christmas and

New Year holidays, were now left with just the clothes on their backs. Almost all of them were in shorts and vests, clutching the bare minimum personal belongings that they could salvage when disaster struck.

Many were still in shock; most had lost their passports, visas, money, and other essentials. I felt sad at the sight, and the full extent of the human suffering suddenly hit me for the first time.

Aircraft from all over the world were coming into land in a continuous stream, to pick up their citizens and fly them home. Large airliners arrived, quickly picked up passengers and left just as quickly as they had come. Slowly, but surely, all the tourists would leave Male, their holiday tragically cut short, but happy to be alive.

Some though, would never make it back home again.

By nightfall, the terminal was empty.

Male had incurred losses close to USD 470 million in the disaster, eighty-two people were killed, twenty-four missing and two-thirds of the capital city was flooded during the first hours of the tsunami. As I watched the last of the planes lifting off, I could not help wondering if anyone from the departing lot would ever return here for a vacation.

The sun set on a forlorn Male that evening.

Meanwhile, our aircraft had been duly refuelled, and we were now all set to return to Thiruvananthapuram.

But the quota of surprises for the day was not done yet. We were suddenly told that the Indian High Commissioner had invited us for dinner at his residence.

Which meant we would be spending the night at Male. The aircraft was secured, and we checked into a hotel. A quick wash and change and we soon found ourselves on a speedboat skimming through the open water at high speed, as it ferried us to our dinner engagement.

The dinner was a simple affair with relaxed, across-the-table conversation with our gracious host. He had offered all possible help to the Male government.

Then came surprise No. 4 of the day. Over dinner, we learnt that the Avros would be staying on in Male for the next few days instead of going back to Thiruvananathapuram as originally planned, to provide relief to the inhabitants of the many far-flung isles of this tiny island nation.

And so, over the next four days, each aircraft flew at least two sorties in a day, often three. We would land at airports we had never heard of before, with difficult to pronounce names like Kadhdhoo, Kaadedhdhoo, and Gan, apart from Hanimadhoo, again.

Barring Male, every airfield had a short runway that required utmost precision in our landings and take-offs. But like before, our pilots took it all in their stride.

Luxury hotels, once the favourite haunts of tourists from all over the globe, lay forlorn and abandoned, in the aftermath of the disaster, as we flew over them. And I could not help reflecting once again, on the fragility of the best laid human plans and endeavours.

And wonder when, if ever, life would return to normalcy in these tiny places, stunning in their splendid isolation, where the world came to unwind and relax.

On 29 December, the third aircraft from our squadron joined us at Male. Unfortunately, the aircraft developed a snag in its landing gear on arrival. The snag in the nose wheel needed urgent repairs without which further landings would be risky. It seemed to us then, that our engineering flight, based at Thiruvananthapuram, would be able to fix the problem.

So the next day, we flew back there in this aircraft.

Upon landing however, we discovered that the problem was much more complex than we had initially thought.

Fortunately spares and expertise were available at Air Force Station, Sulur, just a short flight away, which was the major servicing base for Avro aircraft. We landed there on the evening of 31 December.

The customary New Year Party had been cancelled across all air force bases that year as a mark of respect for tsunami victims; so, it turned out to be a quiet evening as we prepared to wait it out for the repairs to be concluded.

1 January 2005 brought us the good news that our aircraft was serviceable. We quickly did a few ground checks and carried out a few circuits to make sure everything was working fine, and we were good to go.

One of the worst tsunami-affected air force bases at the time was Car Nicobar, the northern-most of the Nicobar Islands. Situated 745 nautical miles into the sea and 150 nautical miles south of Port Blair, this island had suffered heavy casualties, with many houses and buildings washed away.

The sole helicopter unit based there had flown round the clock and saved many lives, but the damage was just too extensive.

Having flown to Car Nicobar many a time in the past, the news coming in from there was heartbreaking.

As part of the relief operations for Car Nicobar or Car Nic, as it was called, several plastic barrels were to be airlifted from Vizag to Port Blair, for onward dispatch there. This had been pending for some days since bad weather and lack of navigational aids at Vizag had made it impossible for aircraft to land there. We were now assigned this task and asked to proceed to Vizag.

Very early next morning, when the rest of the world was still fast asleep, we took off for Vizag, which is a naval airfield with small hills surrounding it on all four sides. At the time, it was not equipped with any navigational aids facilitating approach and landing, and as such, a landing at that airport could be attempted only when visibility was more than 5 km.

We had planned to land there at sunrise, at around 0630 hours, when the weather was expected to be generally clear and the visibility good. Accordingly, we had taken off from Sulur at 0330 hours.

But on arrival over the airport that day, we found a thick layer of clouds that prevented us from sighting the runway. We had no option but to keep orbiting overhead, hoping that the weather would clear up soon. Sure enough, as the sun came up over the eastern seashore, the clouds dissipated, and we could finally make a safe approach for landing at Vizag.

The barrels were quickly loaded, and we were off again, winging our way to Port Blair.

Flying 745 nautical miles out into the open sea with no navigational aids is a challenging task at the best of times. We were depending heavily on fair weather, and good, old-fashioned plotting on the Mercator Charts with the help of the compass and protractor from the Nav bag.

The handheld GPS that we carried at the time was not very reliable and land-based Navaids were not available beyond the first hour into the flight. For the rest of it, pinpointing the aircraft's exact position had to be done manually through calculations taking into account known winds and the distance to fly.

As mentioned earlier, most modern-day aircraft now have in-built GPS, FMS and Inertial Navigation Systems on board, so manual plotting is no longer required and flying over a featureless sea, no longer the challenge that it once was.

But at that time, it was almost like the pioneering seat-of-the-pants flying of the olden days, and we were all painfully aware of stories from World War II, when the B-24 Liberator 'Lady Be Good' miscalculated its headings and distances and headed out over a featureless Sahara Desert instead of turning towards base, till she finally ran out of fuel. The crew bailed out and kept walking in the desert for days, hoping to be picked up.

But tragically, that did not happen.

And there was the B-29 Superfortress that had met with a similar fate over water, and now rests at the bottom of the ocean, where intrepid divers go right down to have a look at its remains.

We did not want to become another footnote in those grim stories and took all possible precautions, as we checked and double checked our distances and headings, to make sure we were on the right course to our destination.

Even so, it was a relief when we finally arrived over Port Blair and landed smoothly, just in time for lunch. The mood at the Base was sombre. They had braved scary, high waves just a few days ago and the tension in the air was still palpable.

Relief operations were by now, fully underway and several passengers were at the airport, waiting to be airlifted back to the mainland. The barrels were quickly off-loaded, and the passenger list was handed over to us by the ground staff. As we went through it, we looked at each other in surprise.

There were fifty-seven names on that list, including women and children.

The Avro's bucket seats could accommodate only about twenty-five people. Carrying all fifty-seven of them would clearly not be possible. We went back to our calculations all over again, this time to determine the maximum safe weight to fly, and thereafter, it would be up to the captain of the aircraft to take the final call.

The majority of the passengers would have to sit on the floor, for the long flight home, if we decided to take them, something usually not recommended or done. But these were clearly, not usual times.

We were still trying to figure out what to do when the passengers started to assemble near the aircraft. There were pregnant women barely able to walk; small, bewildered children clutching rag dolls for comfort; old men with grim, wrinkled faces; and a few from the armed forces, as well. They all had anxiety, despondency and fear writ large on their faces, having just undergone the most traumatic event of their lives. But they looked at us with a hope and expectation that we just did not have the heart to negate. A few moist eyes and tear-stained faces spoke eloquently of the probable loss of near and dear ones.

One look at those faces and the decision was made; we just knew we couldn't possibly leave anyone behind.

Meticulous calculations again—we went right down to each kilogram of weight and once that was sorted, we were ready to go. I carried out the passenger briefing.

'Some of you will be sitting on the floor. Hold on to something during take-off and landing and we will try and avoid turbulence as much as we can,' was all that I could think of saying.

'Don't worry, India is too big to miss, we'll get you home safely,' I added as an afterthought, hoping to raise a smile on those forlorn faces.

Maybe my booming, ex-NDA Appointment Cadet voice gave them some courage and optimism as they quietly settled down for the long flight home. A smooth take-off and we were on our way back to Air Force Station, Tambaram at Chennai.

On a normal day, flying over the sea at night in an Avro was not permitted at the time. But as I said earlier, this was anything but a normal day.

Halfway through the flight, the sun set over the sea in an unforgettable blaze of crimson and gold and soon we were flying through pitch darkness broken only by the comforting, monotonous drone of the propellers churning at a steady 14,200 RPM.

It was back to careful plotting, meticulous airmanship, and accurate flying as we flew on in total darkness over the sea, for what seemed like an eternity.

The passenger cabin was enveloped in total silence.

The mood in the cockpit was equally sombre as the enormity of the human tragedy and loss hit each one of us. No one spoke for a long time.

Finally, when we sighted the lights of Tambaram, we let out a collective whoop of joy in the cockpit, as we prepared to land.

Tambaram also had a short runway back then, barely enough for an Avro, so once again this would be a tricky night landing, especially with the extra load that we were carrying.

But again, the pilots made it look so easy.

We taxied to the brightly lit hangar designated to receive passengers from the Andamans. There were hot cups of coffee and snacks waiting for all of us, as the passengers were met with warmth and empathy. Plans for their onward journey the next day to the respective destinations were worked out amidst much animated discussion and the sense of relief on their faces was worth every bit of the tension of that long, dark journey.

If their despondent silence through the entire flight had been heartbreaking, their animated chatter now, in the hangar, was hugely gratifying for all of us.

We had flown for more than eleven hours that day, one hour more than the prescribed maximum even in 'exceptional circumstances', but we knew only too well that these were not times for rules. As we headed to the Tambaram Officers' Mess looking forward to a hard-earned rest, we felt content.

At the Mess, we found many other crew like us, each with their own stories of relief and rescue. Most of them had stretched themselves and their aircraft to the limits to achieve their tasks.

And all of them felt it was worth every bit of the effort.

Finally, the next day we were on our way home to Vadodara. We dropped off a few passengers at Nagpur en route, and again, their gratitude was gut-wrenching.

The nose wheel was still holding up after the repairs at Sulur, but we did not want to stretch our luck with it, any further. The engineers had cleared it for only five landings and the one at our home base would be the last of the five! We had done all our flying of the last few days on borrowed landing time.

Our aircraft would stay on in Male till 15 February when relief operations finally wound down. Car Nicobar would slowly limp back to normal over time, but the scars and wounds would stay on in people's hearts and minds.

Logbook entries of our sorties show that the three of us had flown a combined 100 hours between 27 December and 3 January. In all humility, this was a phenomenal effort, one that we were very proud of, more so because of the circumstances in which we had operated. As I walked home that evening, I felt a deep sense of gratitude at being allowed to play a small part in this huge relief effort, and touch a few lives with positivity, in their darkest hours.

Today, two decades on, Maldives is once again a bustling holiday destination, thriving and playing host to hordes of holidaymakers on its beaches. But it has taken almost an entire generation to get back there again.

And I often wonder if there is anybody out there today, who is a throwback, a leftover from those dark days, and remembers all that happened back then'.

10

Born and Raised in the IAF (1986–2010)

Looking Back: Experiences in the North-East

On our way to Tawang, across Sela Pass, deep in the Tawang Valley, high up at 10,700 feet, lies Fort Jaswant Garh, where we are told the amazing story of Rifleman, nineteen-year-old Jaswant Singh Rawat, of the Second Garwhal Rifles, who had volunteered to knock out a Chinese MMG (Medium Machine Gun) post that was threatening to decimate his unit, knowing that it meant almost certain death for him. He crawled forward along with two of his mates and threw grenades that silenced the MMG post, killing the gunners manning it. And by doing so, he helped to hold off the Chinese advance, for almost a full day.

The rest of his unit had by then regrouped and fought one of the most valiant battles of the 1962 war, even though a serious head injury meant that he wouldn't live to see that glorious fight-back.

The Army decorated him with a MVC, (Posthumous), the second highest Gallantry Award, and his regiment built a shrine there at the spot where he fought his last battle. Even today, almost every vehicle travelling up that road, stops for a while to pay respects to the young hero. The Army likes to believe that he still lives, a perpetually luminous symbol of bravery and selflessness and all its finest traditions.

These were men who willingly gave up their todays for our tomorrow and it's sad that so few remember or know about them now. Although, in a heartening development, the Government of Arunachal Pradesh, in conjunction with the army, has built memorials and museums to honour these brave men, who fought so valiantly in a forgotten, ill-planned war.

Later we were to visit another war memorial on the slopes of a hill at Kohima in Nagaland, a World War II cemetery, beautifully maintained by the Commonwealth War Graves Commission. Scores of fallen Allied soldiers from World War II lay in neat, orderly rows, amidst flowers in perfectly clipped alpine meadows. Most of them had died heartbreakingly young, trying to block the relentless Japanese advance from Burma, along the Rangoon-Morey-Imphal-Kohima Road. Even today, you still encounter boards proclaiming 'the Japanese advance reached this point on 25 May 1944' etc.

A grim reminder of the days when an entire generation laid down their lives to bring sanity to a world gone mad.

The Kohima War Cemetery lies on the slopes of a hill where the Deputy Commissioner's bungalow was once located, and was the scene of some fierce fighting, including the famous 'Battle of the Tennis Court', where the adversaries faced off, almost literally, on either side of the DC's tennis court, in one of the most decisive battles in that theatre of war. A battle that checked the Japanese advance and turned the tide of the war in favour of the Allies, who pushed on from there, pursuing the retreating Japanese along the Kohima–Imphal road. Bodies of Allied troops moved in from each of these two places, linking up at the historic Milestone 109, ending the Siege of Imphal on 22 June 1943, when the road was finally cleared, and the Japanese driven back into Burma.

Today, a stone tablet commemorates that historic Victory at Kohima, as do some of the epitaphs in the nearby war cemetery.

'Love is like a Bridge that spans the spaces that divide' reads the headstone of a twenty-two-year-old Flight Sergeant of the RAF, 'deeply remembered by devoted wife Nell.' It felt so strange to think that he had been lying there, miles from home, for nearly 80 years now. 'That there's some corner of a foreign field, that is for ever England', as poet Rupert Brooke so poignantly put it . . .

And his wife Nell would now be in her late 90s, if she were still alive.

And what of the story of the old Scottish Bandsman in his 90s, that unfolded before my very eyes at the time when I was posted in the north-east. He flew down all the way there from Bonnie Scotland and played his bagpipes in full uniform at the war cemetery.

For the mates he had left behind in that war, seven decades ago . . .

And how can I possibly forget the headstone that poignantly read, 'To the whole world you were just a soldier, but to us, you were the whole world.'

What does it take for a man to be so fondly remembered, I wonder? What does it take for a man to lay down his life in an alien land, fighting an enemy he has never known, in the name of king and country?

There was none to tell me of course . . . except for another board that said, 'When you go home tell them of us, and say that for your tomorrow we gave our today.'

And I could hear the words of the old Pete Seegar song playing softly in my mind, '. . . *Where have all the Graveyards gone/Gone to Flowers, everyone/Oh, when will they ever learn/ Oh, when will they, ever learn . . .*'

The USAF continued to send out exploratory teams to these areas till a few years ago, trying to locate the remains of their aircraft that perished flying the hump of the Himalayas into China, loaded with men and material.

Searching with ground penetrating radar, for remnants of aircraft that crashed into the densely wooded hillsides of Arunachal, more than seventy years ago, in an effort to bring their airmen home and offer closure to the families.

The Arunachal government is now building a World War II 'Hump' Museum at Pasighat, which used to be one of the ALGs of the IAF.

Later, on another one of our many excursions in Arunachal during my north-eastern tenure at Jorhat in Assam, we came upon a crumbling and forgotten World War II cemetery near Jairampur. The local Assam Rifles unit had stumbled upon it, while clearing the jungle. The mostly unknown graves (the headstones had been destroyed by long years of neglect in the jungle), were of people, some of them non-combatants and labourers, who helped to build the famous Stillwell Road from Ledo in Assam to Burma, and manned logistics supply lines and other administrative positions associated with the war effort.

One of the few, still identifiable, graves was that of a Chinese major.

A board paid tribute to these young, unsung heroes, '. . . who along with the enemy, fought boredom, mosquitoes and disease, heavy rains and squelching mud, to valiantly do their duty in these unforgiving jungles, in the war against fascism.'

We would have never known about them, had I not been in uniform and been posted to these parts.

Notes from the Desert

Moving to a different part of the country on posting, I am off to Phalodi deep in the desert sands of Rajasthan for the first time, from my base at AF Jodhpur, on a cold winter morning that is sunny and misty at the same time, as only these parts can be at this time of the year. Narayan Chowdhary drops me off at the railway station, only to find the intercity express delayed. There are no other trains at this time and it's quiet and peaceful. From the overbridge, I can see the beautiful Mehrangarh fort standing tall on the hill, a familiar blur in the haze, not far from here.

I settle down to wait for my train. My five-year old daughter, who was sleeping when I left, asks me solemnly on the phone, 'tumi ki amay chumu kore giyechile?' (did you kiss me when you left?), and I say, yes, of course, how could I not do that.

A passenger train arrives first, and I get on it, deciding against waiting further for the intercity. It is not crowded, and I find myself a sunny bench near an open window and enjoy the desert views as we pass through the sand dunes at Osian and other tiny railway stations that suddenly spring to life as the train passes through.

Lost amidst a barren, sandy, open landscape that stretches for miles on either side of the railway line.

Three-and-a-half hours later, I get off at Beethri (Marwar) railway station, which is close to the air force camp. A part of the raja's Marwar railway, this has been a train station since 1938 and considering that it's pretty solitary even now, I wonder who it stopped for then, in the middle of this wilderness on all sides? There is a blue Air Force Gypsy waiting to pick me up and by the time we reach the camp, which is still nothing more than a perimeter wall, main gate, watchtowers, and some prefabricated huts where we would be staying, it is lunchtime. I go straight through to the small mess behind my hut and meet the men who are to be my team in this wilderness.

Later in the evening, I set out on a long, lonely trek along the sand-blown perimeter road. From a sand dune, I watch the pink sun slip below the horizon behind the green fields of the village in the distance, touching a low strand of suspended cloud in a sliver of luminescent crimson gold, till long after the sun has set. A sudden quiet and chill descends on the landscape as I pull my jacket closer around myself. My first day in the desert is slowly coming to an end.

A whitish-brown field rat pops out of his hole, rising on his hind legs to get a good look at me. He disappears momentarily and then pops out again successively from a bewildering flurry of interconnected burrows, fast as lightning. His brothers and cousins and sundry other relatives poke their whiskers out of a similar network of burrows. Apparently, the word has spread in the subterranean rat city, and no one wants to miss a look-see at the intruder!

And I find myself wondering where they'll all go when hundreds of men and machines descend on their world.

A startled bunny, camouflaged in the sand by the roadside, scampers away, ears thrown back, bounding away in lifesaving leaps. A family of Nilgais, seven in all, including the young ones, gaze warily at me from a distance, walking a few uneasy steps away, even as small goats rise on their hind legs, straining to reach the green leaves crowning small shrubs. In the distance, tall, majestic camels reach out effortlessly, extending their long necks right up to the top branches of trees painted by the yet-to-set-in spring, in the first coat of tender green.

Next day, the wind howls around the cabin all day, blowing sand into every nook and cranny, into our files and telephones and glasses of water. There is no electricity the whole day, and in this isolated wilderness even my phone doesn't work. If I climb to the top of the nearest watchtower, I shall probably get a bar of mobile signal or so, but with the wind blowing in at gale force from the vast open spaces all around, it is impossible to have any kind of conversation.

I decide to go on a drive around the camp to look at the various work sites. It is bleak and sand-blown, with the gusting winds forming sand dunes at places. Deep sand drifts pile up on the road, making it difficult for any vehicle to pass. My Gypsy gets stuck in one such drift near a watchtower, as the wheels suddenly sink into the sand, and after fifteen minutes of futilely trying to get it out, I decide to trek back to the camp and get help. Our huts are an hour's walk away, but I manage to get back there eventually, and raise a salvage party with a thick rope and our Swaraj Mazda pick-up truck. In no time, we've driven back to the place where the Gypsy floundered, and they've towed the vehicle out. I drive it back to our cabins again and heave a sigh of relief. No damage done, but it's been a lesson for me in desert survival.

And the laugh was definitely on me.

As evening closes in, across the wall, villagers in elaborate headgear herd their sheep and goats back to their 'dhanis' or hut clusters, the days' work done. There is a crop of mustard, bajra, and vegetables in their fields and they have their sheep to get them by, one of them tells me. A rough shawl is all that he wears over his dhoti-kurta to ward off the cold that had gone down to -1.4 degrees last night. 'Day after is Bakri-Id and thirty to forty goats will be slaughtered in the village,' he says as he turns his herd towards Bhom Ki Dhani, which is home to him. 'I will bring you some meat and you need not pay, it's our festival.'

That amazing spirit of giving amongst people who don't really have much to give never fails to tug at my heartstrings.

Back at the hut, night falls on the harsh landscape, bathing it in soft moonlight, miles from anywhere. Sitting alone on the veranda of my little cabin, tucked away amongst the golden sands, I marvel at how bright the stars are—constellations, stars clusters, even the odd shooting star. I'm too overawed to make a wish.

High up, unseen in the skies, a flock of migratory birds fly to an unknown destination, silhouetted against the moon for a moment, their muted cries audible in the quiet stillness of the desert night. I can hear people talking in the distance in unseen villages that are pinpricks of light in the darkness, their voices riding the cold, night air. In that absolute stillness you can perhaps make out what they are saying if you listen closely enough.

After a while, the train tracks running just outside the camp begin to hum. From the distance comes the sound of the approaching night train, one of three that pass through this track in a day. It's miles away yet, ploughing a lonely furrow through the darkness of the vast, open spaces of the desert.

This is a different Rajasthan, far removed from the splendour of the forts and palaces, and the tourists, yet no less fascinating!

Morning brings a beam of soft winter sunshine into the cabin as I step out to meet the winter chill. It feels good to sit in the sun, cup of steaming hot tea in hand, enjoying the warmth of a clear day with just a hint of haze in the desert air, when you can almost see forever.

To the rows of windmills turning languidly in the distance . . .

A few days later, I am back home at Jodhpur for the weekend and sitting on the terrace amongst the plants, enjoying the freshness of the morning. Little Tuli sits next to me with her dolls, softly talking to them.

And I think, maybe I will have some time at home this time, like ma had wished for me, when they visited us at Jodhpur, on what would be the last time they would travel to an Air Force Station from faraway Kolkata.

Till the desert calls again . . .

Images from a Lifetime in the Indian Air Force

Fast forward to 2023. December, my favourite month of the year, has just passed. Those crisp, cold, misty winter mornings that bring with them a hint of holidays and nostalgia. A time to look back, but also look ahead.

And although it's been thirty-seven years now, it seems only yesterday that we fetched up at the Air Force Academy (AFA) one day in early January 1986, a bunch of bright-eyed youngsters with long hair, straight out of college. I still remember the blue-and-white AFA bus that picked us up from outside Secunderabad railway station.

At the Academy, our 'senior course' was waiting, and the long hair was soon gone, as the Academy barber set upon us with relish. A whole new course of flight cadets straight off civvy street—the 79 GDOC as we were called. And in no time, all of us looked the same—a set of dazed, crew-cut zombies who didn't know what had hit them.

One of my course mates, now an Air Commodore, had gone back to the AFA for his son's passing out parade, recently. Incredibly, he found Satya, our barber from a lifetime ago, still holding court at the Cadets Mess barber shop and sent us photographs of the register that he's still kept, recording our haircuts from a lifetime ago. Three regulation haircuts for the month of January 1986, one every ten days, duly signed for and neatly recorded against my name and service number, in the register.

One in forty-five to fifty days is good enough for me now . . . and I guess I am a lot luckier than some!

We blustered and threatened him with dire consequences once we became Officers, but Satya just laughed and snipped away. He wasn't having any of it.

He was a very young man then, probably in his first year of employment like us, which is why he has so lovingly preserved those registers for so long. The records for 78 (our senior course) and 79 GDOC are the only ones that he still has.

I doubt Air HQs would have records that old now, so readily available.

Back in the Cadet's Mess residential blocks, our 'senior' course fell on us with similar relish and cries of '79 GDOC Fall Out' rang out with alarming regularity, by day and night, as we assembled at all hours. Sometimes in drill boots, sometimes in dressing gowns and sometimes in our 'whites and tie'—and did front rolls and haunches and push-ups and star jumps—while our six-month-old 'seniors' stood watchfully by, telling us in all solemnity, that they were trying to make 'soldiers out of us, from the pathetic sissies that we were'.

By the end of the first month of training, we had passed our saluting test and earned the luxury of our first 'book out' to town on a holiday. A whole day to ourselves, to eat out, watch movies and roam around, with no pesky seniors to bother us, even if it was all only in our regulation 'Academy Whites and Tie' and crew cut hair. How we had hoped and prayed that our drill sergeant, Sergeant Andrews would clear us in the first instance and liberate us from the confines of the academy, since without passing the saluting test, you were not permitted to book out and go outside the Academy gate.

We also got to wear our first air force uniforms around this time and felt that we finally belonged.

A month later I was playing in my first Air Force Cricket Championship at Delhi, living out with my elder brother, who was a young Flight Lieutenant then, and sister-in-law, at 57-C Rock View, Air Force Station, Palam. An unheard-of luxury for a junior term flight cadet. Ma, baba and didi had come visiting and it was a much-remembered, much-cherished family reunion for all of us.

My team, Training Command, emerged joint winners that year and I got a good fifty in the final against star-studded Western Air Command (my elder brother was playing for them and predictably, got a hundred), to get selected in the Air Force team. The Commandant of the Air Force Academy, who had been a keen cricketer himself, had let me go on the assurance that when I came back, I would work twice as hard to catch up on the training I'd missed.

By the time I returned to AFA, my seniors eyed me with new-found respect.

Soon it was on to the rigours of the FCTC Camp (Field Craft Training Camp), as we set up residence near Narsapur forest, some distance away from the Academy. Living in tents, wearing overalls and the bowl shaped 'Tommy' helmets of World War II, we went on long marches at night, carrying dummy rifles, maps, and compasses. And woe betide anyone who dared to take a shortcut or hitch a ride with someone—as some of us found out to our cost.

We played soldiers in right earnest, monkey crawling across ropes strung up between trees and crossing imaginary rivers on crazily swaying Burma Bridges, made up of sets of parallel ropes.

And then came the Big Day—6 December 1986—when we were commissioned as young Pilot Officers into the Indian Air Force, proudly wearing the near-invisible, now-extinct single 'quarter inch' stripe on our shoulders. And in one, much-rehearsed handshake with the Chief of Air Staff on the Academy drill square, we transformed from boys to men, from flight cadets to officers. As we glided out in threes in slow march with the Band playing *Auld Lang Syne*, a flight of Polish Iskra fighter jets swung low over our heads, dipping their wings in salute to the newly commissioned officers.

And our Drill Sergeants, who had been so tough with us during our one year of training, stood at attention and gave us our first salutes as we went by. What a moment that was . . .

Life waited. And the world was at our feet, so to say.

Back at the Cadets Mess after the POP, the Passing Out Parade, the CTA, Chief Trainee Administrator, gave us our first pay packets—a princely sum of Rs 2100. Few of us had ever had that kind of money in our pockets before—money we'd earned ourselves! Our monthly allowance as Flight Cadets, had been a miserly Rs 90 till then, sent from home by our parents, and this suddenly felt huge—whatever would we do with it?

We'd all got our posting orders and would soon be moving out to different Air Force Stations. Some of us would not meet again, ever, over the course of our entire service careers. As for me, I was to stay on for another six months at AFA and train to be an Air Traffic Control Officer.

But we had a month's leave first and I was going home to my parents and my friends!

Back then, we used to have the letters DLTGH written at the top right-hand corner of the chalk-and-duster boards in our classrooms. With a number in front that progressively reduced by one, each passing day. It signified 'the number of days left to go home', after the Course.

At the time we were still naive enough to believe that at the end of the course, we'd be done with it all. That we would go back home again after the passing out parade.

But we never really went home after that, ever again—not in any real sense. We just moved on—to our new lives, as our parents watched proudly—going home to them only now and then, on leave.

And that brings back memories of reporting to my first IAF unit as a raw Pilot Officer, fresh out of the Academy. On a Friday afternoon with the weekend looming, I remember taking courage in both hands to call up my Commanding Officer in the ATC from the Main Guard Room, to ask where I should go. I expected to get an earful from a senior officer, the standard response to that question from our senior course cadets at AFA, being a daggers-drawn look and a barked, 'You will find out!'

Instead, how can I ever forget the kindness and warmth with which he asked me to 'get myself down to the Officers Mess' since it was almost the weekend, and that he would meet me there.

And by the time I found my way there, almost all officers of my unit and some of their ladies, had gathered to welcome me, over lunch and a drink, making me feel as if I had always belonged there.

And it was much the same for most young officers, male or female, when they first reported on posting.

A year later, I was playing my first season of Ranji Trophy, under dada's (my elder brother) captaincy. At the workplace, my boss in the ATC had let me go, somewhat reluctantly, on the assurance that I would not ask for leave immediately after I came back, and work hard at picking up my Categorisation (a new ATC officer fresh out of training was Uncategorized or 'UNCAT', which meant that he or she had to be always supervised by a senior, whenever on watch in the Tower).

I made my Ranji trophy debut at Sher-e-Kashmir stadium in Srinagar, against J & K, with our team staying at the Army Transit Camp. Some of my teammates from the Army had joined the side a month earlier, directly from counter-insurgency operations in the Kashmir Valley, or from the icy heights of Siachen Glacier. Some had returned from IPKF (Indian Peace Keeping Force) Operations at Jaffna in Sri Lanka, and most of us had not played cricket in the preceding six months, the last time being at the inter-services championship held at NDA that year, from which the Services team was selected.

In that memorable Ranji Trophy season, almost thirty-six years ago now, a young Flight Lieutenant (my elder brother Bhaskar Ghosh) and an even younger Pilot Officer (me), played for the services against Himachal Pradesh at our home ground, Palam. And we scored Hundreds together in the same innings of a Ranji Trophy match, putting on 179 runs for the second wicket in a classic left-right combo, joining a small list of illustrious brothers who had done that before in first-class cricket, worldwide.

Dada and I have batted together in just four Ranji Trophy matches. So we were really lucky to have had that moment in our lives within that short time. The morning after, we had headlines and our photographs in all major newspapers, as the Ghosh brothers joined some of the most legendary siblings to have graced the game, including the Chappells, Amarnaths, Waughs, Mohammads, Marshes etc.

It was a moment that we remain incredibly proud of, one that we will cherish all our lives, even if there are only a few yellowing newspaper clippings left now, to remind us of it.

Life happened to each one of us in different ways over the years, as our Course picked up service experience and qualifications. Picked up new ranks, new appointments, got married, had families, moved into 'status houses' with gardens from the so-called pigeonholes that we invariably got on initial arrival at a Base. I got posted to different air force stations, from one corner of the country to another, moving every two-and-a-half to three years, accumulating boxes, both wooden and steel, as we packed our lives into them.

And at each new place, there would be a couple of them that remained unopened in our garages, as we acquired new stuff.

Comfortably ensconced in our own little worlds, secure behind Guard Rooms, watchtowers and perimeter walls, the blue uniform was what defined us, shaped our personalities, and made us who we were.

Going home on much-awaited Annual Leaves was a pleasure—you could take the full quota of sixty days at a time if you so wanted—something that the perpetually overworked, forever-busy generation of today cannot even imagine.

The long stays at home made the parting from loved ones almost as excruciatingly difficult as the first time. And I still found it as tough to say goodbye to ma and baba, after more than three decades of going and coming, as on that very first time when I officially left home in December 1985, on my way to the Air Force Academy at Hyderabad with my black trunk (the coffin box as it was called), and a holdall or bedroll!

Holdalls . . . our children wouldn't even know what they were!

The years passed in a whirl . . . our first air experience in an Avro at AFA, as we crowded behind the captain in the cockpit, watching every move as he brought her into land at Santacruz airport. My first ATC 'letdown' with a fighter aircraft in bad weather when visibility was very poor, talking him down on the radio, and the thrill when he crisply said, 'Runway 12 O' clock, thank you' (i.e. visible straight in front), at the end of it. Getting to see and live in some really remote places in the North-East and Ladakh, and in the deserts of Rajasthan, places that we never thought we would see from such close quarters.

Driving up a completely snowbound Sela Pass at 13,700 ft in my Maruti 800 with my young family and three-foot-deep snow on the road. The wheels going into two parallel furrows ploughed by Army bulldozers, even as a fine rain turned to snow amidst gathering darkness, with another three hours to our destination, Tawang, in Arunachal Pradesh.

That was the first time that I'd driven in the hills. And I still remember going up the last seven kilometres to Sela Top in first gear.

Helping to build an Air Force Station in the desert, treks in the hills, flying microlights, including ones where you wore a motorcycle helmet and hung on for dear life to a seat suspended below a colourful delta wing.

Overseas trips with military sports teams. Staying in a 300-year-old manor in the UK, converted to an RAF Officers Mess, where one of the rooms had a ceiling plated with gold. Finding an old grand piano in the Ante Room, on which I played 'purano shei diner kotha' (a much-loved Rabindra sangeet inspired by *Auld Lang Syne*), on a rainy evening when there were few people around.

Till one day, it was time for the big decision to leave and move on to other things. Calling it quits after twenty-four years of commissioned service in the Indian Air Force, the one year as a flight cadet at the Academy not being counted as service. Preparing to move out of the Air Force after nearly twenty-five years in uniform; years that had gone by in a flash.

Only, deep down we all knew we would never actually leave, because the blue uniform, once worn, never really lets you go.

And like at the Academy, it would never quite be **DLTGH 0** for us.

Ever again.

Epilogue

Delhi is so beautiful at this time, with the summer still not set in yet, and winter still clinging on to the early mornings and late evenings. When I took Tuli to Jorbagh for her dance class one Sunday morning, just before our departure, we passed through the wide, tree-lined avenues of Lutyens Delhi, somnolent in the quietness of the dreamy morning—the roundabouts awash in beautifully tended flowers of every conceivable shade and hue.

They had truly *gone to flowers, everyone* . . . as Pete Seegar would say.

Afterwards when I went for a walk in Lodi Gardens, it was the same there as well—neatly mowed lawns and flowers in a mosaic of colour, a feast for the eyes and soul.

This is what I will miss most when I leave Delhi and the Air Force. This part of the city where the rich and the powerful in the higher echelons of government live—in their sprawling, colonial bungalows in quiet, leafy neighbourhoods—relics of a bygone, less tumultuous era.

And the equally leafy and well-tended Cantonments that I had grown used to over the twenty-four years of my work life in the Air Force . . .

But that is life—things change, people move on, adjust to new things.

And I would do the same . . .

Soon it was time for the big moment . . . the emotional farewells as I left my office at Air Force Station, Race Course in the heart of New Delhi for the last time and headed home to Dhaula Kuan Officers Enclave, where I took off my uniform one final time, twenty-five years after I'd first worn it as a Cadet at the Air Force Academy.

I put it on a hanger as I always did—Rank Braids, Name Tab, Ribbons, Commendation Badge, Belt, all neatly in place.

Only, I wouldn't be needing it again . . . I'd lived my Air Force dream.

And it seems that a whole chapter of life has gone by in a flash, and I still can't believe that it was over. It felt like one of our Annual Leave breaks.

That we would go back from when it finished.

Only this time we wouldn't . . .

It was time to hand over the baton to another generation of long-haired, bright-eyed youngsters.

As Life turned the page.

Acknowledgements

This is a book of true stories and first-hand narratives of incidents and events that actually occurred during operations and day-to-day life in the Indian Air Force, spanning nearly a hundred years in its evolution. Most of the references and source information that I have used in this book come from people who lived through those incidents, and from the personal memoirs of a handful of the most legendary personalities of the IAF. There are hundreds of others.

I was fortunate to have spoken to most of them—long conversations, repeated many times—about the events that make up these stories. Although some of them are well into their eighties now, they still remember the past with absolute clarity, as if it all happened yesterday. It was almost as if they could see it unfolding all over again before their eyes as they narrated these remarkable events to me.

I cannot thank each one of them enough—coursemates, old service friends and seniors, and some 'super seniors', who served well before my time in the Air Force. People who opened their hearts and minds to me, as they took a trip down memory lane. In most cases, I have acknowledged their contribution in the text itself. Wherever possible, I have used direct quotes for greater authenticity. Many of these stories are written and built around those conversations for the most part.

Additionally, for gathering detailed factual information to support those conversations, I consulted and reviewed extensive Ministry of Defence reports on the 1962 and 1965 Wars and on the air operations in Kargil. I have looked up resources on IAF history on the Indian Air Force website, and from the archives that were kindly made available to me by the IAF Directorate of Ops (Media). I also perused Wikipedia write-ups on the same.

I have consulted the excellent Bharat Rakshak historical resources on the Indian Air Force on their web portal and researched online newspapers and magazine articles related to some of these stories to improve my understanding of the events. Particularly so, for the chapters called 'Aces High' and 'The Bomber That Flew in from an Aircraft Graveyard'. I was lucky to also speak to some Air Warriors who actually flew those aircraft while in service.

I have looked up details of the 1962 war in that wonderful book *1962: The War That Wasn't* by Shiv Kunal Verma, published in 2016 by Aleph Book Company, and obtained detailed information on the Air War in Kargil from a public domain YouTube video of Air Marshal Raghunath Nambiar, then AOC-in-C, Western Air Command, speaking at an Institute of Defence Studies and Analyses (IDSA) seminar.

I have spoken in great detail to people who manned radar units in the 1971 War and to those who were part of the original Thunderbolts team when it was formed in 1982. And to my coursemate, Group Captain E.K. Prasad, who flew during the tsunami relief operations of 2004. All of these are first-hand accounts acknowledged in the text and I remain ever grateful to them for sharing their experiences with me.

They helped me revive these inspiring tales of long-forgotten events from the glorious history of the IAF in its ninety-second year.

Events that continue to inspire us to this day.

Scan QR code to access the
Penguin Random House India website